Raspberry Pi

Telegram Bot, GPS Module, Flex Sensor, Line Follower Robot, Infrared Sensor, Smart Phone Controlled Home Automation, Motion Sensor Alarm, Torrentbox, Voice Typing on 16x2 LCD etc,...

ANBAZHAGAN K

CONTENTS

Acknowledgments   5

Introduction   6

1. Utilizing Telegram Bot with Raspberry Pi: 7
Sharing Text and Files

2. Raspberry Pi GPS Module Interfacing Tutorial   26

3. Interfacing Flex Sensor with Raspberry Pi   46
utilizing ADC0804

4. Showing Time more than four-Digit seven-   66
Segment Display utilizing Raspberry Pi

5. Line Follower Robot utilizing Raspberry Pi   89

6. Add Infrared Sensor to Raspberry Pi GPIO   109

7. Raspberry Pi based Smart Phone Controlled   120
Home Automation

8. Raspberry Pi Motion Sensor Alarm utilizing   140
PIR Sensor

9. DIY Raspberry Pi Torrentbox: Quickly Turn   147
your Raspberry Pi into an Always on TorrentBox

10. Voice Typing on 16x2 LCD utilizing   164

Raspberry Pi and Android App

ACKNOWLEDGMENTS

The writer might want to recognize the diligent work of the article group in assembling this book. He might likewise want to recognize the diligent work of the Raspberry Pi Foundation and the Arduino bunch for assembling items and networks that help to make the Internet of Things increasingly open to the overall population. Yahoo for the democratization of innovation!

INTRODUCTION

The Internet of Things (IOT) is a perplexing idea comprised of numerous PCs and numerous correspondence ways. Some IOT gadgets are associated with the Internet and some are most certainly not. Some IOT gadgets structure swarms that convey among themselves. Some are intended for a solitary reason, while some are increasingly universally useful PCs. This book is intended to demonstrate to you the IOT from the back to front. By structure IOT gadgets, the per user will comprehend the essential ideas and will almost certainly develop utilizing the rudiments to make his or her very own IOT applications. These included ventures will tell the per user the best way to assemble their very own IOT ventures and to develop the models appeared. The significance of Computer Security in IOT gadgets is additionally talked about and different systems for protecting the IOT from unapproved clients or programmers. The most significant takeaway from this book is in structure the tasks yourself.

1. UTILIZING TELEGRAM BOT WITH RASPBERRY PI: SHARING TEXT AND FILES

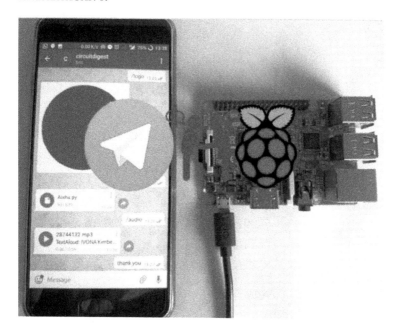

Raspberry Pi has some good times and simple to fabricate ventures. Its ground-breaking ARM design and open-source Linux based Operating System has help us a ton in getting our tasks online right away. In this instructional exercise we will become familiar with another intriguing method to share information (documents/photographs/recordings/sounds/content) between Raspberry Pi and our Mobile telephone through a prevalent talk application called Telegram.

For the individuals who are new to Telegram, it is a talk based application accessible in play store for Android (additionally accessible for Iphone and windows) that is fundamentally the same as Whatsapp. It has more than 100 million downloads (as on 5-10-2017) on play store as well as individuals guarantee it to be quicker and more practical than Whatsapp (fingers crossed). One extraordinary highlights of this application is that they bolster bots. Which means this advanced mobile phone application can not exclusively be utilized by Humans yet in addition by machine. For our situation the machine will be Raspberry Pi. When you train Raspberry Pi on acceptable behavior as a bot, anybody (on the off chance that you cause it open) to can visit with your Raspberry Pi like talking to any typical individual and even offer Photos Pictures Documents and Audio records. You can even prepare it to be your very own collaborator, sounds cool right? Lets figure out how to fabricate a Raspberry pi wire bot.

Materials Required:

- Any Raspberry Pi associated with Internet

- A portable running Telegram Application.

There isn't a lot of equipment engaged with this extend so unwind on your seat with your Pi and pursue the means beneath. On the off chance that you are new to Raspberry Pi, at that point pursue our Raspberry Pi Introduction article and other Raspberry Pi Tutorials.

Note: This instructional exercise accept that your Pi

is as of now associated with web and you realize how to utilize the Lx terminal on you Pi. So associate your Pi to web before continuing.

Stage 1: Installing Telegram on your Mobile

The initial step is introduce Telegram on your Mobile. Wire is accessible for Android, IOS and in any event, for Windows stage so simply feel free to download your Telegram application. Much the same as all application there will be a little Sign Up method to begin utilizing Telegram, proceed with it until you arrive at your home screen.

Step2 : Talk to Bot Father

The subsequent stage is demand the Bot Father to make us another Bot. On the top right corner of the Home screen there will be a hunt symbol, click on it to scan for the name "botfather". Botfather is a Bot without anyone else, it will direct you to make another bot for you. Snap on begin and choose/newbot as appeared in the image beneath. Presently, the bot will request barely any subtleties like name of your Bot and the client name of the bot. Fill those subtleties and recollect the username for we will requiring it in future.

Step3: Getting your token for get to

I have named bot as hello_world as well as the user-name as Hello_worldBot. After this procedure the bot father will give you a Token for get to. This resembles the secret phrase for your bot, individuals can control program your bot utilizing this token key. So keep it safe and don't impart it to anybody. When you have gotten this token key the time has come to proceed onward to Raspberry Pi.

Step4: Telepot for introducing Telegram on Raspberry Pi

Utilizing Telegram Bot in Raspberry Pi is made conceivable by the python bundle called Telepot. We have to introduce this bundle on Raspberry Pi by utilizing the accompanying directions on Lx terminal

```
sudo apt-get install python-pip

sudo pip install telepot
```

Once Telepot is brought into Raspberry we can utilize this bundle in our python program to speak with our Telegram Bot.

Stage 5: Programming your Raspberry Pi

The bot that we just made on Telegram is much the same as an infant, it can't do anything all alone except if we show it what and how to get things done. This educating should be possible through Raspberry Pi and Python content. In this instructional exercise I have modified the bot to play out some fundamental activities like communicating something specific, Photo, Audio and Document. So when you state a specific order it will react with a specific activity the direction and activity is recorded in the table beneath

Command from Telegram	Response by Raspberry Pi
/hi	Replies with a string "Hi! Helloworldbot"
/time	Replies with current time
/logo	Replies with an Image (logo of hiBot)
/file	Replies with a file (that contains current program)
/audio	Replies with a demo audio file

The total program to make the above activities is given at the base of this page. Be that as it may, just beneath, I have clarified the significant pieces in the program to assist you with seeing how the program functions.

The initial step is to import every one of the libraries, here we will clearly require the transport library to utilize the Telegram bot. We additionally utilize the time, timedate library to peruse the present time for Raspberry pi. At that point we make an item now where the worth is put away.

```
import time, datetime

import telepot

from telepot.loop import MessageLoop

now = datetime.datetime.now()
```

The following stage is to make a capacity for taking activities dependent on approaching directions from Telegram application on Mobile. Here the name of the capacity is activity. It is inside this capacity where the bot springs up. Our bot can't start a discussion all alone, it can possibly answer in the event that we ask something. So each time we ask something there will be talk id. This visit id is something like a location, just utilizing this talk id a bot can answer back to us. So the initial step is to peruse the visit id and the message it is attempting to state to us. We additionally print the got message for investigating reason.

```
def action(msg):

    chat_id = msg['chat']['id']
```

```
command = msg['text']

print 'Received: %s' % command
```

Further down inside the capacity we contrast this direction and a predefined message and perform specific assignments. This first order will be/hello there to which we answer "Hey! helloworld"

```
if command == '/hi':

    telegram_bot.sendMessage (chat_id, str("Hi!
Helloworld"))
```

The following direction will be/time, to which we answer the present time. We as of now have the opportunity and date in now, here basically split it dependent on hour and moment and include it as utilizing the str work.

```
elif command == '/time':

    telegram_bot.sendMessage(chat_id,
str(now.hour)+str(":")+str(now.minute))
```

The following direction will be/logo, to which the bot will get a picture from a url and send it to us. A picture can be sent either from a URL or from the hard plate. Here I have quite recently utilized the URL which shows the logo of Helloworld.

```
elif command == '/logo':

    telegram_bot.sendPhoto                (chat_id,
photo="https://i.pinimg.com/avatars/
Helloworld_1464122100_280.jpg")
```

The following order will be/record, which will send the document named Aisha.py from the hard plate. You can send any document that you wish to by changing the location of the catalog

```
elif command == '/file':

    telegram_bot.sendDocument(chat_id, docu-
ment=open('/home/pi/Aisha.py'))
```

The last order will be/sound. This can send any mp3 record from the hard circle, I have recently utilized a sound document called test.mp3 as a demo here

```
elif command == '/audio':

    telegram_bot.sendAudio(chat_id,
audio=open('/home/pi/test.mp3'))
```

Alright currently comes the most significant advance, this is the place we give access of our Telegram bot to the Python content. Here we name out bot as telegram_bot and appoint it the token location that was given by our botfather in stage 3. In the line beneath I have expelled the last hardly any digits of my token as an issue of protection. We additionally utilize the print get me to show the subtleties of the Bot on the shell screen, this will assist us with seeing things working.

```
telegram_bot = telepot.Bot('468382312:AAFhUR-
MxpVlMWEdFzbIQLszBPFEUpXXXXXX')

print (telegram_bot.getMe())
```

Expectation you saw how the program functions, presently let us move to subsequent stage.

Step6: Running the Program in your Raspberry Pi

As said before the total program is given toward the finish of this page, you can likewise download the equivalent from here. When you open the code ensure you change the token location of the program to your token location.

Presently run the python code and you should see the subtleties of your bot on the shell window like this

Here, my bot client name is HelloworldBot. In case you get your bots name here it implies everything is going fine.

When you see "fully operational" it implies that you bot is good to go and would now be able to answer to your directions.

Stage 7: Enjoying the Output

Presently, all that is left is to check how great your bot is reacting for your program. Quest for your bot name for my situation it is "HelloworldBot". Quest for username and not or Bot name, you client name should end with bot.

When you open your bot, click on start and type in any directions like/greetings,/time,/document,/ logo, or/sound and you ought to be answered in like manner.

Note: You may have issue with/sound and/record in the event that you have not changed your catalog to an appropriate document that is accessible on your Raspberry Pi.

You can utilize the shell content to perceive what your content is as of now reacting to.

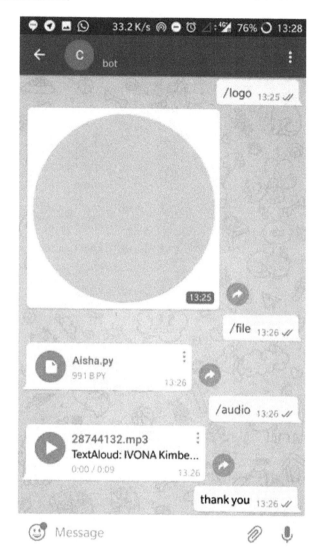

Stage 8: Give me a High Five

Expectation you comprehended the instructional exercise and now will be capable make this Raspberry pi message bot and speak with Raspberry Pi utilizing Telegram App. Too bad! In case you have any issues told me through the remark segment and I will attempt to hit you up. Likewise, let me know how you preferred this task or what you might want me to fabricate utilizing this in up and coming ventures.

Likewise, in our next instructional exercise. We will make this look cooler by changing the manner in which we are sending directions and to something

progressively identified with equipment on Raspberry Pi.

Code

```
import time, datetime
import telepot
from telepot.loop import MessageLoop
now = datetime.datetime.now()
def action(msg):
  chat_id = msg['chat']['id']
  command = msg['text']
  print 'Received: %s' % command
  if command == '/hi':
        telegram_bot.sendMessage (chat_id, str("Hi!
Helloworld"))
  elif command == '/time':
    telegram_bot.sendMessage(chat_id, str(now.hour)
+str(":")+str(now.minute))
  elif command == '/logo':
        telegram_bot.sendPhoto (chat_id, photo =
"https://i.pinimg.com/avatars/helloworld
_1464122100_280.jpg")
  elif command == '/file':
    telegram_bot.sendDocument(chat_id, document-
=open('/home/pi/Aisha.py'))
  elif command == '/audio':
     telegram_bot.sendAudio(chat_id, audio=open('/
home/pi/test.mp3'))
telegram_bot  =  telepot.Bot('468382312:AAFhUR-
```

```
MxpVlMWEdFzbIQLszBPFEUpAeOLFQ')
print (telegram_bot.getMe())
MessageLoop(telegram_bot, action).run_as_thread()
print 'Up and Running....'
while 1:
  time.sleep(10)
```

◆ ◆ ◆

2. RASPBERRY PI GPS MODULE INTERFACING TUTORIAL

One of the coolest inserted stages like the Arduino has enabled creators and DIYers to get area information effectively using Global Positioning System module as well as in this way construct things that depend on area. With the measure of intensity pressed by the Raspberry Pi, it absolutely will be very great to manufacture GPS based activities with the equivalent modest GPS modules and that is the focal point of this post. Today in this venture we will Interface GPS module with Raspberry Pi 3.

The objective of this task is to gather area information (longitude and scope) by means of UART from a GPS module and show them on a 16x2 LCD, so on the off chance that you are curious about the manner in which the 16x2 LCD works with the Raspberry Pi, this is another incredible chance to learn.

Required Components:

- Raspberry Pi 3
- 16 x 2 Liquid Crystal Display
- Neo 6m v2 Global Positioning System Module
- LAN cable to connect the pi to your PC in headless mode
- Power source for the Raspberry Pi
- Resistor / potentiometer to the Liquid Crystal Display
- Breadboard as well as Jumper cables
- Memory card 8 otherwise 16Giga Byte running Raspbian Jessie

Other than that we have to introduce GPS Daemon (GPSD) library, 16x2 LCD Adafruit library, which we introduce later in this instructional exercise.

Here we are utilizing Raspberry Pi 3 with Raspbian Jessie OS. All the essential Hardware and Software necessities are recently examined, you can find it in the Raspberry Pi Introduction.

GPS Module and Its Working:

GPS represents Global Positioning System and used to recognize the Latitude and Longitude of any area on the Earth, with accurate UTC time (Universal Time Coordinated). GPS module is the primary part in our vehicle following framework venture. This gadget gets the directions from the satellite for every single second, with time and date.

GPS module sends the information identified with following situation progressively, and it sends such huge numbers of information in NMEA design (see the screen capture underneath). NMEA position comprise a few sentences, wherein we just need one sentence. This sentence begins from $GPGGA and contains the directions, time and other valuable data. This GPGGA is alluded to Global Positioning System Fix Data. Find out about Reading GPS information and its strings here.

We can extricate arrange from $GPGGA string by including the commas in the string. Assume you discover $GPGGA string and stores it in a cluster, at that point Latitude can be found after two commas and Longitude can be found after four commas. Presently these scope and longitude can be placed in different exhibits.

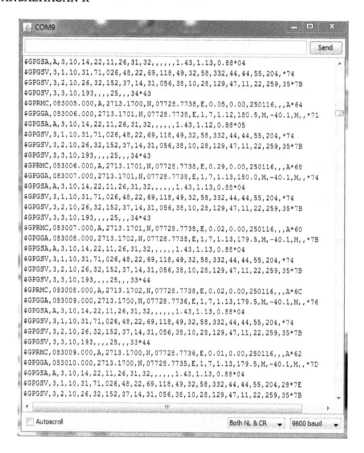

```
$GPGSA,A,3,10,14,22,11,26,31,32,,,,,,1.43,1.13,0.88*04
$GPGSV,3,1,10,31,71,026,48,22,69,118,49,32,58,332,44,44,55,204,*74
$GPGSV,3,2,10,26,32,152,37,14,31,056,38,10,28,129,47,11,22,259,35*7B
$GPGSV,3,3,10,193,,,,,25,,,34*43
$GPRMC,083005.000,A,2713.1700,N,07728.7738,E,0.05,0.00,250116,,,A*64
$GPGGA,083006.000,2713.1701,N,07728.7738,E,1,7,1.12,180.5,M,-40.1,M,,*71
$GPGSA,A,3,10,14,22,11,26,31,32,,,,,,1.43,1.12,0.88*05
$GPGSV,3,1,10,31,71,026,48,22,69,118,49,32,58,332,44,44,55,204,*74
$GPGSV,3,2,10,26,32,152,37,14,31,056,38,10,28,129,47,11,22,259,35*7B
$GPGSV,3,3,10,193,,,,,25,,,34*43
$GPRMC,083006.000,A,2713.1701,N,07728.7738,E,0.29,0.00,250116,,,A*68
$GPGGA,083007.000,2713.1701,N,07728.7738,E,1,7,1.13,180.0,M,-40.1,M,,*74
$GPGSA,A,3,10,14,22,11,26,31,32,,,,,,1.43,1.13,0.88*04
$GPGSV,3,1,10,31,71,026,48,22,69,118,49,32,58,332,44,44,55,204,*74
$GPGSV,3,2,10,26,32,152,37,14,31,056,38,10,28,129,47,11,22,259,35*7B
$GPGSV,3,3,10,193,,,,,25,,,34*43
$GPRMC,083007.000,A,2713.1701,N,07728.7738,E,0.02,0.00,250116,,,A*60
$GPGGA,083008.000,2713.1702,N,07728.7738,E,1,7,1.13,179.5,M,-40.1,M,,*7B
$GPGSA,A,3,10,14,22,11,26,31,32,,,,,,1.43,1.13,0.88*04
$GPGSV,3,1,10,31,71,026,48,22,69,118,49,32,58,332,44,44,55,204,*74
$GPGSV,3,2,10,26,32,152,37,14,31,056,38,10,28,129,47,11,22,259,35*7B
$GPGSV,3,3,10,193,,,,,25,,,33*44
$GPRMC,083008.000,A,2713.1702,N,07728.7738,E,0.02,0.00,250116,,,A*6C
$GPGGA,083009.000,2713.1700,N,07728.7736,E,1,7,1.13,179.5,M,-40.1,M,,*76
$GPGSA,A,3,10,14,22,11,26,31,32,,,,,,1.43,1.13,0.88*04
$GPGSV,3,1,10,31,71,026,48,22,69,118,49,32,58,332,44,44,55,204,*74
$GPGSV,3,2,10,26,32,152,37,14,31,056,38,10,28,129,47,11,22,259,35*7B
$GPGSV,3,3,10,193,,,,,25,,,33*44
$GPRMC,083009.000,A,2713.1700,N,07728.7736,E,0.01,0.00,250116,,,A*62
$GPGGA,083010.000,2713.1700,N,07728.7735,E,1,7,1.13,179.5,M,-40.1,M,,*7D
$GPGSA,A,3,10,14,22,11,26,31,32,,,,,,1.43,1.13,0.88*04
$GPGSV,3,1,10,31,71,026,48,22,69,118,49,32,58,332,44,44,55,204,28*7E
$GPGSV,3,2,10,26,32,152,37,14,31,056,38,10,28,129,47,11,22,259,35*7B
```

The following is the $GPGGA String, alongside its depiction:

$GPG-
GA,104534.000,7791.0381,N,06727.4434,E,1,08,0.
9,510.4,M,43.9,M,,*47

$GPGGA,HHMMSS.SSS,latitude,N,longitude,E,FQ,NOS,HDP,altitude,M,height,M,,checksum information

Identifier	Description
$GPGGA	Global Positioning system fix data
HHMMSS.SSS	Time in hour minute seconds and milliseconds format.
Latitude	Latitude (Coordinate)
N	Direction N=North, S=South
Longitude	Longitude(Coordinate)
E	Direction E= East, W=West
FQ	Fix Quality Data
NOS	No. of Satellites being Used
HPD	Horizontal Dilution of Precision
Altitude	Altitude from sea level
M	Meter
Height	Height
Checksum	Checksum Data

You can check our different GPS ventures:

- Arduino based Vehicle Tracker utilizing GPS and GSM

- Arduino Based Vehicle Accident Alert System utilizing GPS, GSM and Accelerometer

- The most effective method to Use GPS with Arduino

- Track A Vehicle on Google Maps utilizing Arduino, ESP8266 and GPS

Preparing the Raspberry Pi to communicate with GPS:

OK so to bounce in, so this doesn't get exhausting, I will accept you definitely know a great deal about the Raspberry Pi, enough to get your OS introduced, get the IP address, associate with terminal programming like putty and different things about the PI. Should you have any issue doing any of the things referenced above, hit me up under the remark segment and I will be happy to help.

The primary thing we need to do to get this task in progress is to set up our Raspberry Pi 3 to have the option to speak with the GPS module by means of UART, trust me, its very precarious and took a remarkable attempt to take care of business yet in the event that you pursue my guide cautiously you will get it at one go, this is reasonably the most troublesome piece of the venture. Here we have utilized Neo 6m v2 GPS Module.

To make a plunge, here's a little clarification of How the Raspberry Pi 3 UART Works.

The Raspberry Pi has 2 worked in UARTs, a PLO11 as well as a little UART. They are actualized utilizing diverse equipment squares so they have marginally various qualities. On the raspberry pi 3 be that as it may, the remote/bluetooth module is associated with the PLO11 UART, while the smaller than expected UART is utilized for the linux reassure ouptut. Contingent upon how you see it, I will characterize the PLO11 as the best of the two UART because of its usage level. So for this task we will deactivate the Bluetooth module from the PLO11 UART utilizing an overlay accessible in the refreshed current variant of the Raspbian Jessie.

Stage 1: Updating the Raspberry Pi:

The primary thing I like I like to do before beginning each venture is refreshing the raspberry pi. So lets do the standard and run the directions beneath;

```
sudo apt-get update

sudo apt-get upgrade
```

at that point reboot the framework with;

```
sudo reboot
```

Stage 2: Setting up the UART in Raspberry Pi:
The main thing we will do under this is to alter the/ boot/config.txt document. To do this, run the directions underneath:

```
sudo nano /boot/config.txt
```

at the base of the config.txt document, include the accompanying lines

```
dtparam=spi=on

dtoverlay=pi3-disable-bt
```

```
core_freq=250

enable_uart=1

force_turbo=1
```

ctrl+x to exit as well as press y as well as enter to spare.

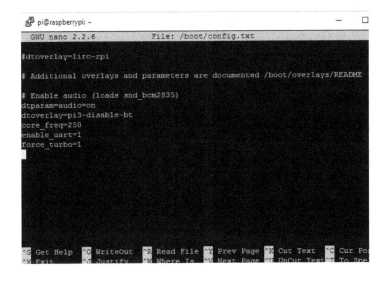

Guarantee there are no mistakes or blunders by two-fold checking as a blunder with this may keep your pi from booting.

What are the purposes behind these directions, force_turbo empowers UART to utilize the most extreme center recurrence which we are setting for this situation to be 250. The explanation behind this is to guarantee consistency and trustworthiness of the sequential information been gotten. Its essential to note now that utilizing force_turbo=1 will void the guarantee of your raspberry pi, yet asides that, its entirely protected.

The dtoverlay=pi3-incapacitate bt separates the bluetooth from the ttyAMA0, this is to permit us access to utilize the full UART control accessible by means of ttyAMA0 rather than the small UART ttyS0.

Second step under this UART arrangement segment is to alter the boot/cmdline.txt

I will recommend you make a duplicate of the cmdline.txt and spare first before altering so you can return to it later if necessary. This should be possible utilizing;

```
sudo    cp    boot/cmdline.txt    boot/cmdline_
backup.txt

sudo nano /boot.cmdline.txt
```

Supplant the substance with;

```
dwc_otg.lpm_enable=0 console=tty1 root=/dev/
mmcblk0p2 rootfstype=ext4 elevator=deadline
fsck.repair=yes rootwait quiet splash plymouth.ig-
nore-serial-consoles
```

Spare and exit.

With this done then we should reboot the framework again to impact changes (sudo reboot).

Step3: Disabling the Raspberry Pi Serial Getty Service

The subsequent stage is to cripple the Pi's sequential the getty administration, the direction will keep it from beginning again at reboot:

```
sudo systemctl stop serial-getty@ttyS0.service

sudo systemctl disable serial-getty@ttyS0.service
```

The accompanying directions can be utilized to empower it again if necessary

```
sudo systemctl enable serial-getty@ttyS0.service
```

```
sudo systemctl start serial-getty@ttyS0.service
```

Reboot the framework.

Stage 4: Activating ttyAMA0:
We have incapacitated the ttyS0, next thing is for us to empower the ttyAMA0.

```
sudo          systemctl          enable          serial-
getty@ttyAMA0.service
```

Step5: Install Minicom as well as pynmea2:

We will be minicom to interface with the Global Positioning System module as well as understand the information. It is likewise one of the apparatuses that we will use to test is our GPS module is working fine. An option to minicom is the daemon programming GPSD.

```
sudo apt-get install minicom
```

To effortlessly parse the got information, we will utilize the pynmea2 library. It tends to be introduced utilizing;

```
sudo pip install pynmea2
```

Library documentation can be found here https://git-hub.com/Knio/pynmea2

Stage 6: Installing the LCD Library:

For this instructional exercise we will utilize the AdaFruit library. The library was made for AdaFruit screens yet in addition works for show sheets utilizing HD44780. In the event that your showcase depends on this, at that point it should work without issues.

I feel its better to clone the library and simply introduce legitimately. To clone run;

```
git      clone      https://github.com/adafruit/
Adafruit_Python_CharLCD.git
```

change into the cloned catalog and introduce it

```
cd ./Adafruit_Python_CharLCD

sudo python setup.py install
```

At this stage, I will recommend another reboot so we are all set on to interfacing the parts.

Connections for Raspberry Pi GPS module Interfacing:

Interface the GPS Module and LCD to the Raspberry Pi as appeared in the Circuit Diagram beneath.

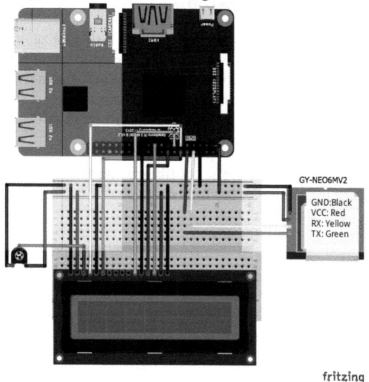

GY-NEO6MV2

GND:Black
VCC: Red
RX: Yellow
TX: Green

fritzing

Testing before Python Script:

I feel its critical to test the GPS module association before continuing to the python content, We will utilize minicom for this. Run the order:

sudo minicom -D/dev/ttyAMA0 -b9600

where 9600 speaks to the baud rate at which the GPS module conveys. This might be utilized for once we make certain of information correspondence between the GPS and the RPI, its opportunity to compose our python content.
The test should likewise be possible utilizing feline

sudo cat /dev/ttyAMA0

```
pi@raspberrypi:- $ clear
pi@raspberrypi:- $ sudo cat /dev/ttyAMA0

$GPGLL,0649.0846,N,00327.1015,E,172206.000,A,A*5B

$GPGSA,A,3,09,06,19,23,28,03,22,30,01,17,,,2.0,0.9,1.8*3B

$GPGSV,3,1,12,01,17,147,17,02,09,322,,03,23,085,17,06,50,320,31*7A

$GPGSV,3,2,12,07,74,060,,09,30,011,30,17,28,218,24,19,30,244,20*7A

$GPGSV,3,3,12,22,11,103,15,23,13,035,28,28,17,176,18,30,66,194,28*73

$GPRMC,172206.000,A,0649.0846,N,00327.1015,E,0.00,102.80,021017,,,A*62

$GPVTG,102.80,T,,M,0.00,N,0.00,K,A*36

$GPZDA,172206.000,02,10,2017,00,00*51

$GPTXT,01,01,01,ANTENNA OK*35

$GPGGA,172207.000,0649.0846,N,00327.1016,E,1,10,0.9,57.6,M,0.0,M,,*50

$GPGLL,0649.0846,N,00327.1016,E,172207.000,A,A*59
```

In Window, you can see NMEA sentences which we have talked about before.

Python Script for this Raspberry Pi GPS instructional exercise is given underneath in Code segment.

With all said and done, its opportunity to test the entire framework. Its significant that you guarantee your GPS is getting a decent fix, by taking it out, most GPS require between three to 4 satellites to get a fix, despite the fact that mine worked indoor.

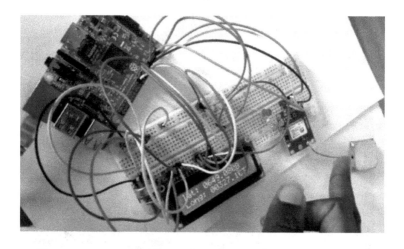

Works Right? Yea...

Have questions or remarks? Drop them in the remark segment.

We have indicated the Location in scope and longitude on LCD utilizing GPS and Raspberry Pi.

Code

```
import time
import serial
import string
import pynmea2
import RPi GPIO as gpio
#to add the LCD library
import Adafruit_CharLCD as LCD
gpio.setmode(gpio.BCM)
#declaring LCD pins
lcd_rs = 17
lcd_en = 18
lcd_d4 = 27
lcd_d5 = 22
lcd_d6 = 23
lcd_d7 = 10
lcd_backlight = 2
lcd_columns = 16 #Lcd column
lcd_rows = 2 #number of LCD rows
lcd = LCD.Adafruit_CharLCD(lcd = LCD.Adafruit_CharLCD(lcd_rs, lcd_en, lcd_d4, lcd_d5, lcd_d6, lcd_d7, lcd_columns, lcd_rows, lcd_backlight)
port = "/dev/ttyAMA0" # the serial port to which the pi is connected.
#create a serial object
ser = serial.Serial(port, baudrate = 9600, timeout =
```

```
0.5)
while 1:
  try:
    data = ser.readline()
  except:
print("loading")
#wait for the serial port to churn out data
  if data[0:6] == '$GPGGA': # the long and lat data are
always contained in the GPGGA string of the NMEA
data
    msg = pynmea2.parse(data)
#parse the latitude and print
    latval = msg.lat
concatlat = "lat:" + str(latval)
    print concatlat
lcd.set_cursor(0,0)
lcd.message(concatlat)
#parse the longitude and print

longval = msg.lon
concatlong = "long:"+ str(longval)
print concatlong
lcd.set_cursor(0,1)
lcd.message(concatlong)
  time.sleep(0.5)#wait a little before picking the next
data.
```

3. INTERFACING FLEX SENSOR WITH RASPBERRY PI UTILIZING ADC0804

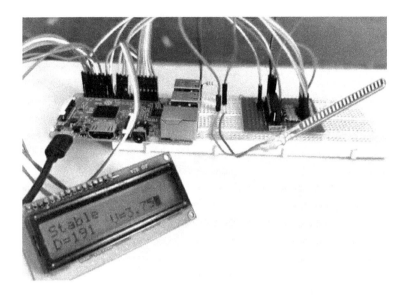

Raspberry Pi is an ARM design processor based board intended for electronic specialists and specialists. The PI is one of most confided in venture improvement stages out there now. With higher processor speed as well as 1 Giga Byte Random Access Memory, the PI can be utilized for some, prominent activities like Image preparing and Internet of Things. There are a ton of cool things that should be possible with a PI, however one tragic element is that it doesn't have an inbuilt ADC module.

Just, if the Raspberry Pi could be interfaced with sensors it can become acquainted with about this present reality parameters and associate with it. The greater part of the sensors out there are simple sensor and henceforth we ought to figure out how to utilize an outer ADC module IC with Raspberry Pi to interface these sensors. In this task we will figure out how we would interface be able to Flex Sensor with Raspberry Pi as well as Display its Values on LCD Screen.

Material Required:

- Raspberry Pi (Any Model)
- 16*2 LCD display
- ADC0804 IC
- Resistors and capacitors
- Flex Sensor
- Breadboard otherwise perf board.

ADC0804 Single Channel 8-bit ADC module:

Before we continue any further, let us find out about this ADC0804 IC and how to utilize this with raspberry pi. ADC0804 is a solitary channel 8-piece IC, which means it can peruse a solitary ADC worth and guide it to 8-piece of computerized information. These 8-piece advanced information can be perused by the Raspberry Pi, in this way the worth will be 0-255 since 2^8 is 256. As appeared in the pinouts of the IC underneath, the pins DB0 to DB7 are utilized to peruse these computerized qualities.

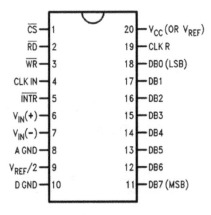

Presently another significant thing here is, the ADC0804 works at 5V thus it gives yield in 5V rationale sign. In 8 pin yield (speaking to 8bits), each pin gives +5V yield to speak to rationale '1'. So the issue is the PI rationale is of +3.3v, so you can't give +5V rationale to the +3.3V GPIO pin of PI. On the off chance that you offer +5V to any GPIO pin of PI, the board gets harmed.

So to step-down rationale level from +5V, we will utilize voltage divider circuit. We have talked about Voltage Divider Circuit already investigate it for further explanation. What we will do is, we utilize two resistors to partition +5V rationale into 2*2.5V rationales. So after division we will give +2.5v rationale to Raspberry Pi. In this way, at whatever point rationale '1' is introduced by ADC0804 we will see +2.5V at the PI GPIO Pin, rather than +5V. Become familiar with ADC here: Introduction to ADC0804.

The following is the image of ADC Module utilizing ADC0804 that we have based on Perf Board:

Circuit Diagram and Explanation:

The total circuit outline for interfacing Flex Sensor with Raspberry Pi is demonstrated as follows. The clarification of the equivalent is as per the following.

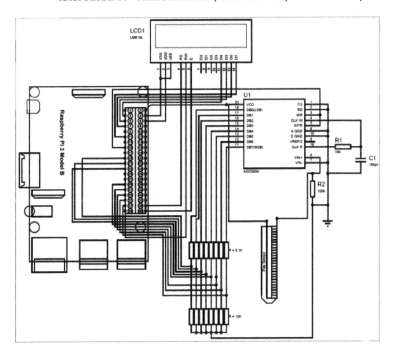

This raspberry pi flex sensor circuit may appear to be somewhat unpredictable with bunches of wires, however in case you investigate the majority of the wires are straightforwardly associated from the LCD and 8-piece information pin to the Raspberry pi. The accompanying table will support you while making and confirming the associations.

Pin name	Raspberry Pin number	Raspberry Pi GPIO name
LCD Vss	Pin 4	Ground

LCD Vdd	Pin 6	Vcc (+5V)
LCD Vee	Pin 4	Ground
LCD Rs	Pin 38	GPIO 20
LCD RW	Pin 39	Ground
LCD E	Pin 40	GPIO 21
LCD D4	Pin 3	GPIO 2
LCD D5	Pin 5	GPIO 3
LCD D6	Pin 7	GPIO 4
LCD D7	Pin 11	GPIO 17
ADC0804 Vcc	Pin 2	Vcc (+5V)
ADC0804 B0	Pin 19 (through 5.1K)	GPIO 10
ADC0804 B1	Pin 21 (through 5.1K)	GPIO 9
ADC0804 B2	Pin 23 (through 5.1K)	GPIO 11
ADC0804 B3	Pin 29 (through 5.1K)	GPIO 5
ADC0804 B4	Pin 31 (through 5.1K)	GPIO 6
ADC0804 B5	Pin 33 (through 5.1K)	GPIO 13
ADC0804 B6	Pin 35 (through 5.1K)	GPIO 19
ADC0804 B7	Pin 37 (through 5.1K)	GPIO 26

ADC0804 WR/ INTR	Pin 15	GPIO 22

You can utilize the accompanying picture to decide the pin numbers on Raspberry since.

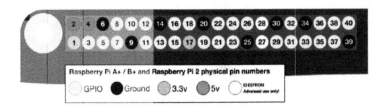

Like all ADC modules, the ADC0804 IC additionally requires a clock sign to work, fortunately this IC has an inward clock source, so we simply need to add the RC circuit to the CLK in and CLK R sticks as appeared in the circuit. We have utilized an estimation of 10K and 105pf, however we can utilize any worth close like 1uf, 0.1uf, 0.01uf ought to likewise work.

At that point to interface the Flex sensor we have utilized a potential divider circuit utilizing a 100K resistor. As the Flex sensor is bowed the opposition crosswise over it will change thus will the potential drop over the resistor. This drop is estimated by the ADC0804 IC and 8-piece information is produced appropriately.

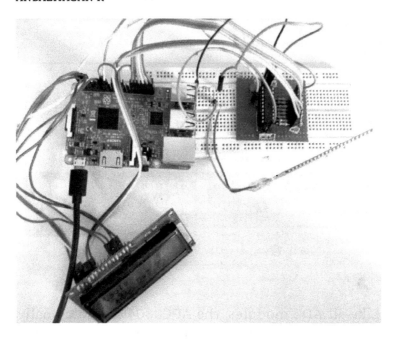

Check different undertakings identified with Flex Sensor:

- Flex Sensor Interfacing with AVR Microcontroller

- Arduino based Angry Bird Game Controller utilizing Flex Sensor

- Servo Motor Control by Flex Sensor

- Creating Tones by Tapping Fingers utilizing Arduino

Programming the Raspberry Pi:

When we are finished with the associations, we should peruse the status of these eight-bits utilizing Raspberry Pi as well as convert them to Decimal so we can utilize them. The program for doing likewise and showing the subsequent qualities on the LCD screen is given at the end of this page. Further the code is clarified into little throws out beneath.

We need a LCD library to interface LCD with Pi. For this we utilize the library created by shubham which will push us to interface a 16*2 LCD show with a Pi in four wire mode. Likewise we require libraries to utilize time as well as Pi GPIO pins.

Note: The lcd.py ought to be downloaded from here, and put in a similar registry where this program is spared. At exactly that point the code will order.

```
import lcd #Import the LCD library by shubham@
electro-passion.com

import time #Import time

import RPi.GPIO as GPIO #GPIO will be reffered as
GPIO only
```

The LCD pin definitions are alloted to the factors as demonstrated as follows. Note that these numbers are the GPIO pin numbers and not the genuine pin numbers. You can utilize the table above to contrast GPIO numbers and pin numbers. The exhibit paired will incorporate every one of the information pin numbers and the cluster bits will store the subsequent estimation of all the GPIO pins.

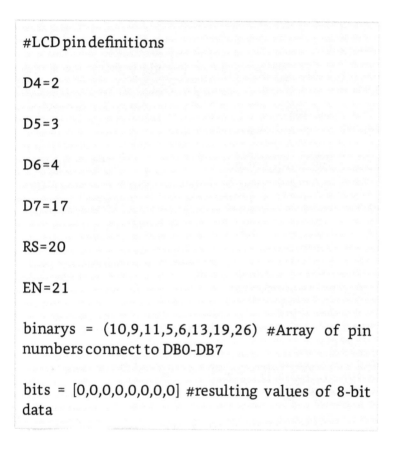

```
#LCD pin definitions

D4 = 2

D5 = 3

D6 = 4

D7 = 17

RS = 20

EN = 21

binarys = (10,9,11,5,6,13,19,26) #Array of pin numbers connect to DB0-DB7

bits = [0,0,0,0,0,0,0,0] #resulting values of 8-bit data
```

Presently, we need to characterize the information

and yield pins. The seven information pins will be the info pin and the trigger pin (RST and INTR) will be the yield pin. We can peruse the 8-piece information esteems from input pin just in the event that we trigger the yield pin high for a specific time as indicated by the datasheet. Since we have announced the double pins in binarys cluster we can utilize a for circle for statement as demonstrated as follows.

```
for binary in binarys:

    GPIO.setup(binary, GPIO.IN) #All binary pins are input pins

  #Trigger pin

    GPIO.setup(22, GPIO.OUT) #WR and INTR pins are output
```

Presently utilizing the LCD library directions we can instate the LCD module and show a little introduction message as demonstrated as follows.

```
mylcd=lcd.lcd()

mylcd.begin(D4,D5,D6,D7,RS,EN)
```

```
#Intro Message

mylcd.Print("Flex Sensor with")

mylcd.setCursor(2,1)

mylcd.Print("Raspberry Pi")

time.sleep(2)

mylcd.clear()
```

Inside the unending while circle, we start perusing the double qualities convert them to decimal and update the outcome on LCD. As said before we read the ADC esteems we should make the trigger pin to be high for a specific time to actuate the ADC transformation. This is finished by utilizing the accompanying lines.

```
GPIO.output(22, 1) #Turn ON Trigger

time.sleep(0.1)

GPIO.output(22, 0) #Turn OFF Trigger
```

Presently, we should peruse the 8-information pins and update the outcome in the bits exhibit. To do this we utilize a for circle to contrast each information pin and True and False. In case genuine the separate bits cluster will be made as 1 else it will be made as 0. This was all the 8-piece information will be made 0 and 1 individual of the qualities read.

```
#Read the input pins and update result in bit array

    for i in range(8):

        if(GPIO.input(binarys[i]) == True):

            bits[i] = 1

        if(GPIO.input(binarys[i]) == False):

            bits[i] = 0
```

When we have refreshed the bits cluster, we should change over this exhibit to decimal worth. This is only paired to decimal transformation. For 8-piece parallel information 2^8 is 256. So we will get decimal information since 0 to 255. In python the administrator "*" is utilized to discover the intensity of any worth. Since bits[0] begins with MSB we increase it with 2^(7-position). Thusly we can change over all the paired qualities to decimal information and afterward show it on the LCD

```
#calculate the decimal value using bit array

    for i in range(8):

    decimal = decimal + (bits[i] * (2**(7-i)))
```

When we know the decimal worth it is anything but difficult to figure the voltage esteem. We simply need to duplicate it with 19.63. Since for a 8-piece 5VADC each piece is a similarity of 19.3 milli volt. The subsequent voltage esteem is the estimation of voltage that has showed up over the pins Vin+ and Vin-of the ADC0804 IC.

```
#calculate voltage value

    Voltage = decimal * 19.63 *0.001 #one unit is
    19.3mV
```

Utilizing the estimation of voltage we can decide how the flex sensor has been twisted and in what heading it has been bowed. In the underneath lines I have quite recently contrasted the perused voltage esteems and foreordained estimations of voltage to show the situation of the Flex sensor on the LCD screen.

```
#compare voltage and display status of sensor

        mylcd.setCursor(1,1)

    if(Voltage>3.8):

        mylcd.Print("Bent Forward")

    elif(Voltage<3.5):

        mylcd.Print("Bent Backward")

    else:

        mylcd.Print("Stable")
```

Additionally you can utilize the voltage incentive to play out any assignment that you wish the Raspberry Pi to perform.

Showing Flex Sensor value on LCD using Raspberry Pi:

The working of the task is straightforward. Be that as it may, ensure you have installed the lcd.py header record and have set it in a similar catalog where your present program is available. At that point make the associations are appeared in the circuit outline utilizing a breadboard or a perf board and run the underneath program on your Pi and you ought to get thing working. You set up should look something like this beneath.

As demonstrated the LCD will show the Decimal worth, voltage worth and sensor position. Simply twist the sensor forward or in reverse and you ought to have the option to see the voltage and decimal worth getting differed, likewise a status content will be shown. You can interface any sensor and notice the Voltage crosswise over it getting fluctuated.

Expectation you comprehended the task and delighted in building something comparable.

Code

```
import lcd #Import the LCD library by electro-pas-
sionindia
import time #Import time
import RPi.GPIO as GPIO #GPIO will be referred as
GPIO only
GPIO.setmode(GPIO.BCM)
GPIO.setwarnings(False)
#LCD pin definitions
D4=2
D5=3
D6=4
D7=17
RS=20
EN=21
binarys = (10,9,11,5,6,13,19,26) #Array of pin num-
bers connect to DB0-DB7
bits = [0,0,0,0,0,0,0,0] #resulting values of 8-bit data
for binary in binarys:
    GPIO.setup(binary, GPIO.IN) #All binary pins are
input pins
 #Trigger pin
    GPIO.setup(22, GPIO.OUT) #WR and INTR pins are
output
mylcd=lcd.lcd()
mylcd.begin(D4,D5,D6,D7,RS,EN)
#Intro Message
mylcd.Print("Flex Sensor with")
mylcd.setCursor(2,1)
```

```
mylcd.Print("Raspberry Pi")
time.sleep(2)
mylcd.clear()
while 1:
  decimal = Voltage = 0 #intitialize to zero
  GPIO.output(22, 1) #Turn ON Trigger
  time.sleep(0.1)
  GPIO.output(22, 0) #Turn OFF Trigger
  mylcd.clear()
#Read the input pins and update result in bit array
  for i in range(8):
    if(GPIO.input(binarys[i]) == True):
      bits[i] = 1
    if(GPIO.input(binarys[i]) == False):
      bits[i] = 0
#print binary values if required for debugging
##  mylcd.Print("Binary= ")
##  mylcd.setCursor(1,8)
##  for i in range(8):
##    mylcd.Print(bits[i])
  #calculate the decimal value using bit array
for i in range(8):
    decimal = decimal + (bits[i] * (2**(7-i)))
#Display decimal value
  mylcd.setCursor(2,1)
  mylcd.Print("D=")
  mylcd.setCursor(2,3)
  mylcd.Print(decimal)
#calculate voltage value
    Voltage = decimal * 19.63 *0.001 #one unit is
19.3mV
```

```
#compare voltage and display status of sensor
mylcd.setCursor(1,1)
 if(Voltage>3.8):
   mylcd.Print("Bent Forward")
 elif(Voltage<3.5):
   mylcd.Print("Bent Backward")
 else:
   mylcd.Print("Stable")
 Voltage = str(round(Voltage,2)) #limit to two digit
after decimal
 #display voltage
mylcd.setCursor(2,8)
 mylcd.Print("V=")
 mylcd.setCursor(2,10)
 mylcd.Print(Voltage)
 time.sleep(0.5) #relaxing time
```

◆ ◆ ◆

4. SHOWING TIME MORE THAN FOUR-DIGIT SEVEN-SEGMENT DISPLAY UTILIZING RASPBERRY PI

We as a whole realize that Raspberry Pi is a magnificent Development stage dependent on ARM microchip. With its high computational power it can work out miracles in hands of hardware specialists or understudies. This can be conceivable just in case we realize how to cause it to associate with this present reality and investigate the information through some yield gadget. There are numerous sensors which can identify certain parameters from the constant world and move it to a computerized world and we break down them seeing them either in a LCD screen or some other presentation. However, it would consistently be not conservative to utilize a LCD screen with PI for showing modest quantity of information. This is the place we like to utilize 16x2 Alphanumeric LCD show or the 7-Segment show. We have as of now figured out how to utilize an Alphanumeric LCD and a solitary fragment 7-portion show with Raspberry pi. Here we will Interface four-digit 7 Segment Display Module with Raspberry Pi as well as show Time over it.

Albeit 16x2 Alphanumeric LCD is considerably more agreeable than 7-fragment show, there are scarcely any situations where a 7-section show would come in handier than a LCD show. LCD experiences the downside of having low character size and will be needless excess for your venture in the event that you are simply intending to show some numeric qualities. 7-sections likewise have the preferred position against poor lighting condition and can be seen from ale points than an ordinary LCD screen. Along these lines, let us start knowing it.

7-Segment and 4-Digit 7-Segment Display Module:

Seven Segment Display has 7 sections in it as well as each fragment has 1 LED inside it to show the numbers by illuminating the comparing portions. Like on the off chance that you need the 7-fragment to show the number "5" at that point you have to shine section a,f,g,c, and d by making their comparing pins high. There are 2 sorts of 7-section shows: Common Cathode and Common Anode, here we are utilizing Common Cathode seven portion show. Study 7 section show here.

Presently we realize how to show our ideal numeric character on a solitary 7-portion show. In any case, it is quite apparent that we would require more than one 7-fragment show to pass on any data that is more than one digit. Along these lines, in this instructional exercise we will utilize a 4-digit 7-Segment Display Module as demonstrated as follows.

As should be obvious there are 4 7 Segment Displays associated together. We realize that every 7-portion module will have 10 pins and for 4 seven section shows there would be 40 pins altogether and it would be rushed for anybody to bind them on a speck board, so I would energetically prescribe anybody to purchase a module or make your very own PCB for utilizing a 4-digit 7-fragment show. The association schematic for the equivalent is demonstrated as below:

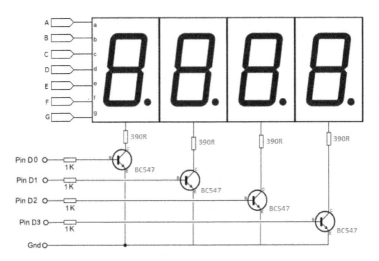

To see how 4-digit seven portion module functions we need to investigate the above schematics, as indicated the A pins of every one of the four showcase is associated with accumulate as one An and the equivalent for B,C.... upto DP. Things being what they are, fundamentally in case trigger An on, at that point every one of the four An's ought to go high right?

Be that as it may, that doesn't occur. We have extra four pins from D0 to D3 (D0, D1, D2 as well as D3) which can be utilized to control which show out of the four ought to go high. For instance: If I need my yield to be available just on the second show then just D1 ought to be made high while keeping different pins (D0, D2, and D3) as low. Just we can choose which show needs to go dynamic utilizing the pins from D0 to D3 and what character to be show utilizing the pins from A to DP.

Connecting 4-digit 7-segment module with Raspberry Pi:

Give us a chance to perceive how, how we can interface this 4-digit 7-fragment module with our Raspberry Pi. The 7-section module has 16 pins as demonstrated as follows. You module may have lesser, however don't stress it will in any case have the accompanying without a doubt

- 7 or 8 section pins (here pins beginning from 1 to 8)

- Ground pin (here pin 11)

- 4 digit pins (here pins 13 to 16)

Underneath given is the schematic for raspberry pi computerized clock by interfacing 4-digit Seven fragment show module with Raspberry Pi:

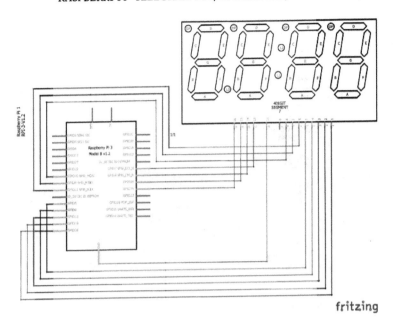

fritzing

The accompanying table will likewise help you in making the associations and checking it to be according to the schematics appeared previously.

S.No	Rsp Pi GPIO number	Rsp Pi PIN number	7-Segment name	7-Seg pin number (here in this module)
1	GPIO 26	PIN 37	Segment a	1
2	GPIO 19	PIN 35	Segment b	2
3	GPIO 13	PIN 33	Segment c	3
4	GPIO 6	PIN 31	Segment d	4
5	GPIO 5	PIN 29	Segment e	5
6	GPIO 11	PIN 23	Segment f	6
7	GPIO 9	PIN 21	Segment g	7
8	GPIO 10	PIN 19	Segment DP	8

ANBAZHAGAN K

9	GPIO 7	PIN 26	Digit 1	13
10	GPIO 8	PIN 24	Digit 2	14
11	GPIO 25	PIN 22	Digit 3	15
12	GPIO 24	PIN 18	Digit 4	16
13	Ground	Ground	Ground	11

Distinguish the pins on your module and you are generally great to continue with the associations. Recognizing the GPIO sticks in Raspberry pi may be somewhat testing assignment so I have given you this image to GPIO Pins.

Programming your Raspberry Pi:

Here we are utilizing Python Programming language for programming RPi. There are numerous approaches to program your Raspberry Pi. In this instructional exercise we are utilizing the Python 3 IDE, since it is the most utilized one. The total Python program is given toward the finish of this instructional exercise. Get familiar with Program and run code in Raspberry Pi here.

We will discuss not many directions which we are going to use in PYHTON program for this venture,
First we are going to import GPIO record from library, underneath work empowers us to program GPIO pins of PI. We are likewise renaming "GPIO" to "IO", so in the program at whatever point we need to allude to GPIO pins we will utilize the word 'IO'. We have likewise imported time and datetime to peruse the estimation of time from Rsp Pi.

```
import RPi.GPIO as GPIO

import time, datetime
```

Now and again, when the GPIO pins, which we are attempting to utilize, may be doing some different capacities. All things considered, we will get admonitions while executing the program. Underneath order advises the PI to overlook the alerts and continue with the program.

```
IO.setwarnings(False)
```

We can allude the GPIO pins of PI, either by nail number to board othrewise by their capacity number. Like 'PIN 29' on the board is 'GPIO5'. So we advise here it is possible that we will speak to the pin here by '29' or '5'. GPIO.BCM implies we will speak to utilizing 5 for GPIO5 pin 29.

```
IO.setmode (GPIO.BCM)
```

As consistently we should start by initialising the pins, here both the portion pins and the digit pins are yield pins. For programming reason we structure exhibits for fragment sticks and instate them to '0' subsequent to proclaiming them as GPIO.OUT

```
segment8 = (26,19,13,6,5,11,9,10)

for segment in segment8:
```

```
GPIO.setup(segment, GPIO.OUT)

GPIO.output(segment, 0)
```

So also for the digit pins we pronounce them as yield pins and make them '0' as a matter of course

```
#Digit 1

GPIO.setup(7, GPIO.OUT)

GPIO.output(7, 0) #Off initially

#Digit 2

GPIO.setup(8, GPIO.OUT)

GPIO.output(8, 0) #Off initially

#Digit 3

GPIO.setup(25, GPIO.OUT)

GPIO.output(25, 0) #Off initially

#Digit 4

GPIO.setup(24, GPIO.OUT)
```

```
GPIO.output(24, 0) #Off initially
```

We need to shape exhibits to show each number on a seven portion show. To show one number we need to control every one of the 7 section pins (speck pin avoided), that is they either must be killed or turned on. For instance to show the number 5 we have make the accompanying game plan

S.No	Rsp Pi GPIO number	7-Segment name	Status to display '5'. (0-> OFF, 1->ON)
1	GPIO 26	Segment a	1
2	GPIO 19	Segment b	1
3	GPIO 13	Segment c	0
4	GPIO 6	Segment d	1
5	GPIO 5	Segment e	1
6	GPIO 11	Segment f	0
7	GPIO 9	Segment g	1

So also we have arrangement number for all numbers and letters in order. You can compose without anyone else or utilize the diagram beneath.

Number	g f e d c b a	Hexadecimal
0	0 1 1 1 1 1 1	3F
1	0 0 0 0 1 1 0	06
2	1 0 1 1 0 1 1	5B
3	1 0 0 1 1 1 1	4F
4	1 1 0 0 1 1 0	66
5	1 1 0 1 1 0 1	6D
6	1 1 1 1 1 0 1	7D
7	0 0 0 0 1 1 1	07
8	1 1 1 1 1 1 1	7F
9	1 1 0 1 1 1 1	6F

With these information we can shape the clusters for each number in our python program as demonstrated as follows.

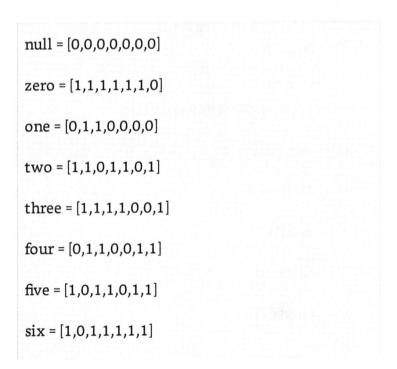

null = [0,0,0,0,0,0,0]

zero = [1,1,1,1,1,1,0]

one = [0,1,1,0,0,0,0]

two = [1,1,0,1,1,0,1]

three = [1,1,1,1,0,0,1]

four = [0,1,1,0,0,1,1]

five = [1,0,1,1,0,1,1]

six = [1,0,1,1,1,1,1]

```
seven = [1,1,1,0,0,0,0]

eight = [1,1,1,1,1,1,1]

nine = [1,1,1,1,0,1,1]
```

In case you pursue the program there will be a capacity to show each character to our 7-portion show in any case, lets skirt this until further notice and get into the while boundless circle. Where perused the here and now from Raspberry Pi and split the estimation of time between four factors. For instance in the event that the time is 10.45, at that point the variable h1 will have 1, h2 will have 0, m1 will have 4vand m2 will have 5.

```
now = datetime.datetime.now()

hour = now.hour

minute = now.minute

h1 = hour/10

h2 = hour % 10

m1 = minute /10
```

```
m2 = minute % 10

print (h1,h2,m1,m2)
```

We need to show these four variable qualities on our four digits separately. To compose an estimation of variable to a digit we can utilize the accompanying lines. Here we are show on digit 1 by causing it to go high then the capacity print_segment (variable) will be called to show the incentive in factor on the section show. You may be asking why we have a deferral after that and why we turn this digit off after this.

```
GPIO.output(7, 1) #Turn on Digit One

print_segment (h1) #Print h1 on segment

time.sleep(delay_time)

GPIO.output(7, 0) #Turn off Digit One
```

The explanation is, as we probably am aware we can show just a single digit at once, yet we have four digits to be shown and just if all the four digits are shown the total four digit number will be obvious for the client.

Things being what they are, how show every one of

the 4 digits simultaneously?

Fortunate for us our MPU is especially quicker than a human eye, so what we really do: we show each digit in turn yet we do it quick as appeared previously.

We select one digit show it sit tight for 2ms (variable delay_time) so the MPU and 7-section can process it and afterward turn off that digit and proceed onward to the following digit and do likewise till we arrive at the last digit. This postponement of 2ms can't be seen by a human eye and all the four digits give off an impression of being ON simultaneously.

The exact opposite thing to learn it to know how the print_segment(variable) work works. Inside this capacity we utilize the exhibits that we have pronounced up until now. So whatever variable that we send to this capacity ought to have the incentive between (0-9), the variable character will get this worth and analyze it for genuine worth. Here the variable is contrasted and '1'. So also we contrast with all number from 0 with 9. In case it is a match we utilize the clusters and allot each an incentive to its separate section sticks as demonstrated as follows.

```
def print_segment(charector):

    if charector == 1:
```

```
for i in range(7):

    GPIO.output(segment8[i], one[i])
```

Display time on 4-Digit 7-segment using Raspberry Pi:

Utilize the schematic and code offered here to make the associations and program your raspberry pi as needs be. In the wake of everything is done simply dispatch the program and you should locate the present time being shown in the seven section show. In any case, there are scarcely any things that you need to check before this

- Ensure you have set your Raspberry Pi with current time to be safe on the off chance that it running on disconnected time.

- Power your Raspberry pi with an Adapter and not with your Laptop/PC in light of the fact that the measure of current drawn by the 7-section show is high and your USB port can't source it.

In the event that everything is functioning true to form, at that point you should discover something like this beneath.

Expectation you preferred the venture and delighted in building one.

Code

```
import RPi.GPIO as GPIO
import time, datetime
now = datetime.datetime.now()
GPIO.setmode(GPIO.BCM)
GPIO.setwarnings(False)


#GPIO ports for the 7 seg pins
segment8 = (26,19,13,6,5,11,9,10)


for segment in segment8:
  GPIO.setup(segment, GPIO.OUT)
```

```python
GPIO.output(segment, 0)


  #Digit 1
GPIO.setup(7, GPIO.OUT)
GPIO.output(7, 0) #Off initially
#Digit 2
GPIO.setup(8, GPIO.OUT)
GPIO.output(8, 0) #Off initially
#Digit 3
GPIO.setup(25, GPIO.OUT)
GPIO.output(25, 0) #Off initially
#Digit 4
GPIO.setup(24, GPIO.OUT)
GPIO.output(24, 0) #Off initially
null = [0,0,0,0,0,0,0]
zero = [1,1,1,1,1,1,0]
one = [0,1,1,0,0,0,0]
two = [1,1,0,1,1,0,1]
three = [1,1,1,1,0,0,1]
four = [0,1,1,0,0,1,1]
five = [1,0,1,1,0,1,1]
six = [1,0,1,1,1,1,1]
seven = [1,1,1,0,0,0,0]
eight = [1,1,1,1,1,1,1]
nine = [1,1,1,1,0,1,1]
def print_segment(charector):
  if charector == 1:
    for i in range(7):
      GPIO.output(segment8[i], one[i])
```

```python
if charector == 2:
    for i in range(7):
        GPIO.output(segment8[i], two[i])
if charector == 3:
    for i in range(7):
        GPIO.output(segment8[i], three[i])
if charector == 4:
    for i in range(7):
        GPIO.output(segment8[i], four[i])
if charector == 5:
    for i in range(7):
        GPIO.output(segment8[i], five[i])
if charector == 6:
    for i in range(7):
        GPIO.output(segment8[i], six[i])
if charector == 7:
    for i in range(7):
        GPIO.output(segment8[i], seven[i])
if charector == 8:
    for i in range(7):
        GPIO.output(segment8[i], eight[i])
if charector == 9:
    for i in range(7):
        GPIO.output(segment8[i], nine[i])
if charector == 0:
    for i in range(7):
        GPIO.output(segment8[i], zero[i])


    return;
```

```python
while 1:
  now = datetime.datetime.now()
  hour = now.hour
  minute = now.minute
  h1 = hour/10
  h2 = hour % 10
  m1 = minute /10
  m2 = minute % 10
  print (h1,h2,m1,m2)



  delay_time = 0.001 #delay to create virtual effect



   GPIO.output(7, 1) #Turn on Digit One
  print_segment (h1) #Print h1 on segment
  time.sleep(delay_time)
  GPIO.output(7, 0) #Turn off Digit One
  GPIO.output(8, 1) #Turn on Digit One
  print_segment (h2) #Print h1 on segment
  GPIO.output(10, 1) #Display point On
  time.sleep(delay_time)
  GPIO.output(10, 0) #Display point Off
  GPIO.output(8, 0) #Turn off Digit One
  GPIO.output(25, 1) #Turn on Digit One
  print_segment (m1) #Print h1 on segment
  time.sleep(delay_time)
  GPIO.output(25, 0) #Turn off Digit One
```

```
GPIO.output(24, 1) #Turn on Digit One
print_segment (m2) #Print h1 on segment
time.sleep(delay_time)
GPIO.output(24, 0) #Turn off Digit One

    #time.sleep(1)
```

5. LINE FOLLOWER ROBOT UTILIZING RASPBERRY PI

As we as a whole know Raspberry Pi is a great Developing stage dependent on ARM chip. With its high computational power and improvement choices it can work out marvels in hands of gadgets specialists or understudies. To become familiar with a Raspberry Pi and how it functions, let us take a stab at building a Line Follower Robot utilizing Raspberry Pi.

In case you are keen on apply autonomy, at that point you ought to be acquainted with the name "Line Follower Robot". This robot is fit for following a line, just by utilizing couple of sensor as well as engines. It probably won't sound productive to utilize a ground-breaking chip like Raspberry Pi to fabricate a straightforward robot. In any case, this robot gives you space for limitless advancement and robots like Kiva (Amazon distribution center robot) are a model for this. You can likewise check our other Line Follower Robots:

- Line Follower Robot utilizing 8051 Microcontroller

- Line Follower Robot utilizing Arduino

Materials Required:

- Raspberry Pi 3 (any model should work)

- DC Gear Motor (2Nos)

- IR Sensor (2Nos)

- Chaises (You can likewise assemble your own utilizing cardboards)

- L293D Motor Driver

- Power bank (Any accessible power source)

Concepts of Line Follower

Line Follower Robot can follow a line with the assistance of an IR sensor. This sensor has an IR Transmitter as well as IR beneficiary. The IR transmitter (IR LED) transmits the light as well as the Receiver (Photodiode) trusts that the transmitted light will return back. An IR light will return back just in the event that it is reflect by a surface. Though, all surfaces don't mirror an IR light, just white the shading surface can totally reflect them and dark shading surface will totally watch them as appeared in the figure underneath. Get familiar with IR sensor module here.

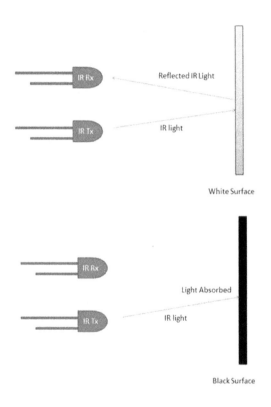

White Surface

Black Surface

IR Sensor Module

Presently we will utilize two IR sensors to check if the robot is in track with the line and two engines to address the robot if its moves out of the track. These engines require high ebb and flow and ought to be bi-directional; consequently we utilize an engine driver module like L293D. We will likewise require a computational gadget like Raspberry Pi to educate the engines dependent on the qualities from the IR sensor. A streamlined square chart of the equivalent is demonstrated as follows.

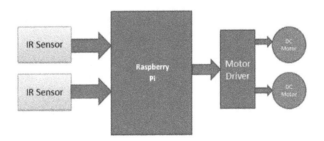

These two IR sensors will be set one on either side of the line. In case none of the sensors are recognizing a dark line them they PI teaches the engines to push ahead as demonstrated as follows

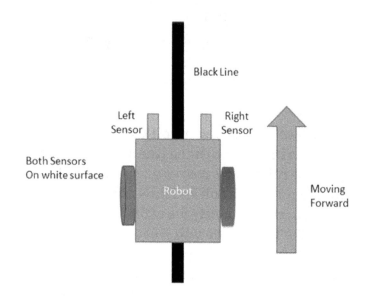

Whenever left sensor goes ahead dark line then the PI educates the robot to turn left by pivoting the correct wheel alone.

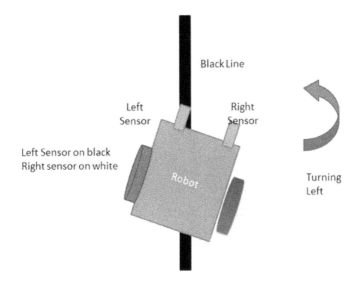

On the off chance that correct sensor goes ahead dark line, at that point the PI teaches the robot to turn directly by pivoting the disregarded wheel.

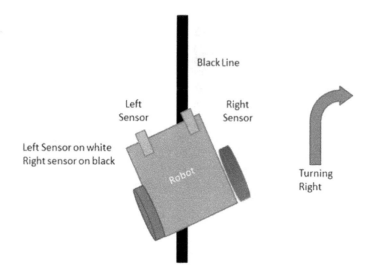

In the event that the two sensors goes ahead dark line, robot stops.

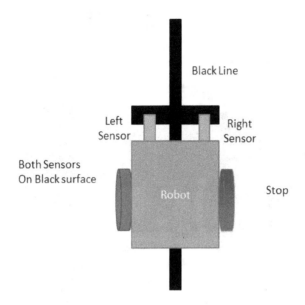

Thusly the Robot will have the option to pursue the line without getting outside the track. Presently let us perceive how the circuit and Code resembles.

Raspberry Pi Line Follower Robot Circuit Diagram and Explanation:

The total circuit graph for this Raspberry Pi Line Follower Robot is demonstrated as follows

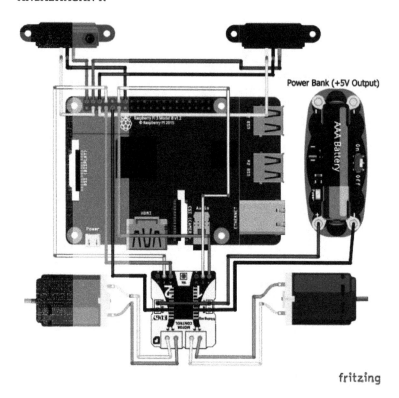

Power Bank (+5V Output)

fritzing

As should be obvious the circuit includes two IR sensor and a couple of engines associated with the Raspberry pi. The total circuit is controlled by a Mobile Power bank (spoke to by AAA battery in the circuit above).

Since the pins subtleties are not referenced on the Raspberry Pi, we have to confirm the pins utilizing the beneath picture

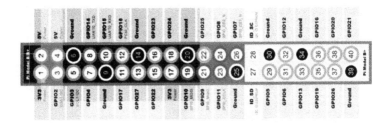

As appeared in the image the upper left corner pin of the PI is the +5V pin, we utilize this +5V pin to control the IR sensors as appeared in the circuit chart (red wired). At that point we interface the ground pins to the ground of the IR sensor and Motor Driver module utilizing dark wire. The yellow wire is utilized to interface the yield pin of the sensor 1 and 2 to the GPIO pins and 3 individually.

To drive the Motors, we need four pins (A,B,A,B). This four pins are associated from GPIO14,4,17 and 18 separately. The orange and white wire together structures the association for one engine. So we have two such matches for two engines.

The engines are associated with the L293D Motor Driver module as appeared in the image as well as the driver module is controlled by a power bank. Ensure that the ground of the power bank is associated with the ground of the Raspberry Pi, at exactly that point your association will work.

Programming your Raspberry PI:

When you are finished with your get together and associations your robot should look something like this.

Presently, the time has come to program our bot and make it run. The total code for this bot can be found at the base of this instructional exercise. Get familiar with Program and run code in Raspberry Pi here. The significant lines are clarified beneath

We are gonna to import GPIO record from library, beneath work empowers us to program GPIO pins of PI. We are additionally renaming "GPIO" to "IO", so in the program at whatever point we need to allude to GPIO pins we will utilize the word 'IO'.

```
import RPi.GPIO as IO
```

Now and again, when the GPIO pins, which we are attempting to utilize, may be doing some different capacities. All things considered, we will get alerts while executing the program. Underneath order advises the PI to disregard the alerts and continue with the program.

```
IO.setwarnings(False)
```

We can allude the GPIO pins of PI, either by nail number to board otherwise by their capacity number. Like 'PIN 29' on the board is 'GPIO 5'. So we advise here it is possible that we will speak to the pin here by '29' or '5'.

```
IO.setmode (IO.BCM)
```

We are setting 6 pins as info/yield pins. The initial two pins are the information pins to peruse the IR sensor. The following four are the yield sticks out of which initial two is utilized to control the correct engine and the following two for the left engine.

```
IO.setup(2,IO.IN) #GPIO 2 -> Left IR out

IO.setup(3,IO.IN) #GPIO 3 -> Right IR out

IO.setup(4,IO.OUT) #GPIO 4 -> Motor 1 terminal A

IO.setup(14,IO.OUT) #GPIO 14 -> Motor 1 terminal B

IO.setup(17,IO.OUT) #GPIO 17 -> Motor Left terminal A

IO.setup(18,IO.OUT) #GPIO 18 -> Motor Left terminal B
```

The IR sensor yields "Genuine" on the off chance that it is over a white surface. So as long as both the sensor says True we can push ahead.

```
if(IO.input(2)==True    and    IO.input(3)==True):
#both white move forward

    IO.output(4,True) #1A+

    IO.output(14,False) #1B-

    IO.output(17,True) #2A+

    IO.output(18,False) #2B-
```

We need to make a correct turn if the main IR sensor comes over a dark line. This is finished by perusing he IR sensor and if condition is fulfilled we stop the correct engine and turn disregarded engine as appeared in the code underneath

```
elif(IO.input(2)==False   and   IO.input(3)==True):
#turn right

    IO.output(4,True) #1A+

    IO.output(14,True) #1B-

    IO.output(17,True) #2A+
```

```
IO.output(18,False) #2B-
```

We need to make a left turn if the second IR sensor comes over a dark line. This is finished by perusing he IR sensor and if condition is fulfilled we stop the left engine and turn right engine alone as appeared in the code underneath

```
elif(IO.input(2)==True and IO.input(3)==False): #turn left

    IO.output(4,True) #1A+

    IO.output(14,False) #1B-

    IO.output(17,True) #2A+

    IO.output(18,True) #2B-
```

In the event that both the sensor comes over a dark line, it implies that the robot needs to stop. This should be possible by making both the terminals of the engine to be valid as appeared on the code beneath

```
else: #stay still
```

```
IO.output(4,True) #1A+

IO.output(14,True) #1B-

IO.output(17,True) #2A+

IO.output(18,True) #2B-
```

Raspberry Pi Line Follower in Action:

Transfer the python code for line supporter to your Raspberry Pi and run it. We need a compact power supply, a power bank for this situation becomes helpful henceforth I have utilized the equivalent. The one that I am utilizing accompanies two USB ports so I have used to control the PI and other to Power Motor Driver as appeared in the image beneath.

Presently all that you require to do is set up your very own dark shading track and discharge your bot over it. I have utilized a dark shading Insulation tape to make the track you can utilize any dark shading material, yet ensure your ground shading isn't dull.

Expectation you comprehended the task and delighted in building one.

Code

```
import RPi.GPIO as IO
import time
IO.setwarnings(False)
IO.setmode(IO.BCM)

IO.setup(2,IO.IN) #GPIO 2 -> Left IR out
IO.setup(3,IO.IN) #GPIO 3 -> Right IR out
```

```
IO.setup(4,IO.OUT) #GPIO 4 -> Motor 1 terminal A
IO.setup(14,IO.OUT) #GPIO 14 -> Motor 1 terminal B
IO.setup(17,IO.OUT) #GPIO 17 -> Motor Left terminal A
IO.setup(18,IO.OUT) #GPIO 18 -> Motor Left terminal B
while 1:
  if(IO.input(2)==True and IO.input(3)==True): #both while move forward
    IO.output(4,True) #1A+
    IO.output(14,False) #1B-
    IO.output(17,True) #2A+
    IO.output(18,False) #2B-
      elif(IO.input(2)==False and IO.input(3)==True): #turn right
    IO.output(4,True) #1A+
    IO.output(14,True) #1B-
    IO.output(17,True) #2A+
    IO.output(18,False) #2B-
      elif(IO.input(2)==True and IO.input(3)==False): #turn left
    IO.output(4,True) #1A+
    IO.output(14,False) #1B-
    IO.output(17,True) #2A+
    IO.output(18,True) #2B-
    else: #stay still
    IO.output(4,True) #1A+
    IO.output(14,True) #1B-
    IO.output(17,True) #2A+
```

IO.output(18,True) #2B-

6. ADD INFRARED SENSOR TO RASPBERRY PI GPIO

As we as a whole know Raspberry Pi is a superb Developing stage dependent on ARM microchip. With its high computational power it can work out marvels in hands of gadgets specialists or understudies. This can be conceivable just in case we realize how to cause it to collaborate with this present reality. There are numerous sensors which can identify certain parameters from the ongoing scene and move it to an advanced world. We have secured part of Raspberry Pi Projects with numerous sensors. Raspberry Pi is additionally an aid for IoT ventures, as it is a pocket estimated PC with inbuilt Wi-Fi, having capacities of a microcontroller.

In this instructional exercise we will figure out how we can Interface an IR sensor with Raspberry pi. These sensors are most normally use in little robots like line supporter robot, Edge staying away from robot and so forth.. Essentially putting, it can distinguish the nearness of articles before it and furthermore separate among white and dark shading. Sounds cool right?

So lets figure out how to interface this sensor with Raspberry Pi. In this task, when there is no item before IR sensor then the Red LED stays turned on and soon as we put something before IR sensor then red LED kills and Green LED turn on. This circuit can likewise fill in as Security Alarm Circuit.

Material Required:

- Raspberry Pi three (any model)
- Green as well as Red Light Emitting Diode lights
- InfraRed sensor Module
- Connecting wires
- Breadboard

IR Sensor Module:

IR sensors (Infrared sensor) are modules which recognize the nearness of items before them. In case the article is available it give 3.3V as yield and in case it is absent it gives 0 volt. This is made conceivable by utilizing a couple of IR pair (transmitter and collector), the transmitter (Infrared Light Emitting Diode) will emanate an IR beam which will get reflected if there is an item present before it. This IR beam will be gotten back by the beneficiary (Photodiode) and the yield will be made high after enhanced utilizing an operation amp interface LM358. You can get familiar with IR Sensor Module Circuit here.

The IR Sensor utilized in this task is appeared previously. Like all IR sensor it has 3 pins which are 5V, Gnd as well as Out separately. The module is controlled by the 5V pin from Raspberry Pi and the out pin is associated with GPIO14 of Raspberry Pi. The potentiometer over the module can be utilized to change the scope of the IR sensor.

Circuit Diagram and Explanation:

The circuit graph for interfacing Raspberry Pi with IR sensor is demonstrated as follows. As should be obvious the circuit chart is straightforward. We have legitimately controlled the IR module from the 5V and Ground Pin of Raspberry Pi. The yield pin of the IR module is associated with the GPIO14. We have likewise utilized two LED (Green and Red) to show the status of the item. These two LEDs are associated with GPIO 3 and GPIO 2 individually.

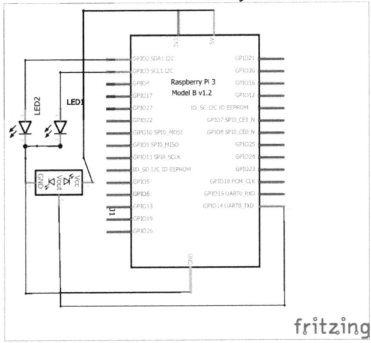

Since the GPIO pins of Raspberry Pi are 3.3 V, a present restricting resistor isn't required. Be that as it may whenever wanted a resistor of significant worth 470 ohms can be included between the ground pin of LEDs and Raspberry Pi. The entire circuit is fueled by a 5V versatile charger through the miniaturized scale USB port of the Raspberry pi.

Note: When associating any sensor, ensure the ground of the sensor is associated with ground of the MCU or MPU (here Raspberry Pi). At exactly that point they will have the alternative to impart.

Programming your Raspberry Pi:

Here we are utilizing Python Programming language for programming RPi. There are numerous approaches to program your Raspberry Pi. Here we are utilizing the Python 3 IDE, since it is the most utilized one. The total Python program is given toward the finish of this instructional exercise. Get familiar with Program and run code in Raspberry Pi here.

We will discuss not many directions which we are going to use in PYHTON program,

We are going to import GPIO document from library, beneath work empowers us to program GPIO pins of PI. We are additionally renaming "GPIO" to "IO", so in the program at whatever point we need to allude to GPIO pins we will utilize the word 'IO'.

```
import RPi.GPIO as IO
```

At times, when the GPIO pins, which we are attempting to utilize, may be doing some different capacities. All objects deemed, we will get admonitions while executing the program. Underneath order advises the PI to overlook the alerts and continue with the program.

```
IO.setwarnings(False)
```

We can allude the GPIO pins of PI, by nail number to board otherwise by their capacity number. Like 'PIN 29' at the board is 'GPIO 5'. So we advise here it is possible that we will speak to the pin here by '29' or '5'.

```
IO.setmode (IO.BCM)
```

We are setting 3 pins as info/yield pins. The two yield pins will control the LED and the info pin will peruse signal from the IR sensor.

```
IO.setup(2,IO.OUT) #GPIO 2 -> Red LED as output

IO.setup(3,IO.OUT) #GPIO 3 -> Green LED as output

IO.setup(14,IO.IN) #GPIO 14 -> IR sensor as input
```

Presently we need to kill the Green LED and turn on the Red LED when the article is far. This should be possible by checking the GPIO 14 pin.

```
if(IO.input(14)==True): #object is far away

    IO.output(2,True) #Red led ON

    IO.output(3,False) # Green led OFF
```

Also we need to turn on the Green LED and mood killer the Red LED when the article is close.

```
if(IO.input(14)==False): #object is near

    IO.output(3,True) #Green led ON

    IO.output(2,False) # Red led OFF
```

Beneath order is utilized as always circle, with this direction the announcements inside this circle will be executed consistently.

```
While 1:
```

Working:

When you have made your python code, execute it

utilizing the run direction. In case the program is executed with no mistakes you ought to get the accompanying screen.

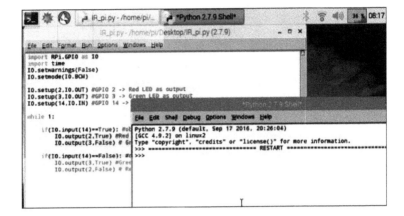

You ought to likewise observe the red shading LED going high when there is no article before the sensor as demonstrated as follows.

Presently, carry something near the IR drove and you should see the red LED killing and the Green turning on.

Expectation you comprehended the task and had the option to assemble something helpful with it.

Code

```
import RPi.GPIO as IO
import time
IO.setwarnings(False)
IO.setmode(IO.BCM)
IO.setup(2,IO.OUT) #GPIO 2 -> Red LED as output
IO.setup(3,IO.OUT) #GPIO 3 -> Green LED as output
```

```
IO.setup(14,IO.IN) #GPIO 14 -> IR sensor as input
while 1:
  if(IO.input(14)==True): #object is far away
    IO.output(2,True) #Red led ON
    IO.output(3,False) # Green led OFF


  if(IO.input(14)==False): #object is near
    IO.output(3,True) #Green led ON
    IO.output(2,False) # Red led OFF
```

7. RASPBERRY PI BASED SMART PHONE CONTROLLED HOME AUTOMATION

Raspberry Pi is exceptionally well known for IoT ventures as a result of its consistent capacity of remote correspondence over web. Raspberry Pi 3 has inbuilt Wi-Fi and Bluetooth, and Bluetooth is an extremely famous remote correspondence Protocol. So we are gonna to Manage Home Appliances through Smart Phone utilizing Raspberry Pi three as well as Bluetooth.

Here we are utilizing Raspberry Pi 3 which have inbuilt Bluetooth, so we don't have to utilize any outside USB Bluetooth dongle. Aside from that we just

need Relay Modules for this Wireless Home Automation Project. Here we are utilizing RFCOMM Bluetooth convention for remote correspondence.

Programming for Bluetooth in Python pursues the attachment programming model and correspondences
between the Bluetooth gadgets is done through RF-
COMM attachment. RFCOMM (Radio Frequency Communication) is a Bluetooth Protocol which gave imi-
tated RS-232 sequential ports and furthermore called
as Serial Port Emulation. Bluetooth sequential port
profile depends on this convention. RFCOMM is exceptionally prevalent in Bluetooth applications as a
result of its wide help and publically accessible API. It
is bound to L2CAP convention.

In case you have Raspberry Pi 2, at that point you
either need to utilize outer Bluetooth dongle or Bluetooth module HC-06. Check our past undertakings for
utilizing these outer Bluetooth gadgets: Controlling
Raspberry Pi GPIO utilizing Android App over Bluetooth and Voice controlled LEDs utilizing Raspberry
Pi. Likewise check our past Raspberry Pi Projects
alongside some great IoT Projects.

**Installing Required Packages for Bluetooth Commu-
nication:**

Prior to begin, we have to introduce a few virtual
products for setting up Bluetooth correspondence in
Raspberry Pi. You ought to have a Raspbian Jessie

introduced memory card prepared with Raspberry Pi. Check this article to introduce the Raspbian OS and beginning with Raspberry Pi. So now we first need to refresh the Raspbian utilizing underneath directions:

```
sudo apt-get update

sudo apt-get upgrade
```

At that point we have to introduce not many Bluetooth related bundles:

```
sudo apt-get install bluetooth blueman bluez
```

At that point reboot the Raspberry Pi:

```
sudo reboot
```

BlueZ is an open source task and authority Linux Bluetooth convention stack. It bolsters all the center Bluetooth conventions and now become piece of authentic Linux Kernel.

Blueman gives the Desktop interface to oversee and

control the Bluetooth gadgets.

At last we need python Library for Bluetooth correspondence with the goal that we can send and get information through RFCOMM utilizing Python language:

```
sudo apt-get install python-bluetooth
```

Likewise introduce the GPIO bolster libraries for Raspberry Pi:

```
sudo apt-get install python-rpi.gpio
```

Presently we are finished with introducing required bundles for Bluetooth correspondence in Raspberry Pi.

Pairing Devices with Raspberry Pi over Bluetooth:

Matching Bluetooth Devices, similar to cell phone, with Raspberry Pi is extremely simple. Here we have matched our Android Smart telephone with Raspberry Pi. We have recently introduced BlueZ in Pi, which gives a direction line utility called "bluetooth-ctl" to deal with our Bluetooth gadgets.

Presently open the bluetoothctl utility by underneath order:

```
sudo bluetoothctl
```

You can check every one of the directions of bluetoothctl utility by composing 'help'. Until further notice we have to enter underneath directions in given request:

```
[bluetooth]# power on

[bluetooth]# agent on

[bluetooth]# discoverable on

[bluetooth]# pairable on

[bluetooth]# scan on
```

After the keep going order "examine on", you will see your Bluetooth gadget (Mobile telephone) in the rundown. Ensure that your versatile has Bluetooth turned on and obvious by close by gadgets. At that point duplicate the MAC address of you gadget and pair it by utilizing given direction:

```
pair <address of your phone>
```

At that point you will be incited for Passcode or Pin in your Terminal support at that point type password there and press enter. At that point type the equivalent password in your cell phone when provoked and you are currently effectively combined with Raspberry Pi.

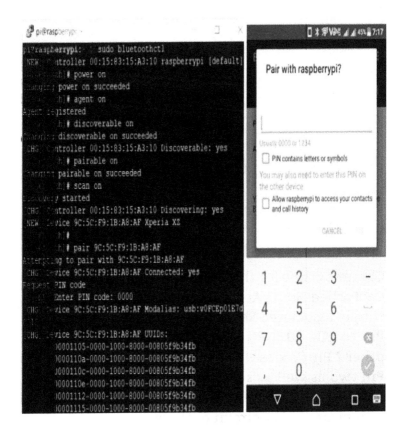

As told before, you can likewise utilize Desktop interface to combine the Mobile telephone. Subsequent to introducing Blueman, you will see a Bluetooth symbol in right half of your Raspberry Pi work area as demonstrated as follows, utilizing which you can undoubtedly do the blending.

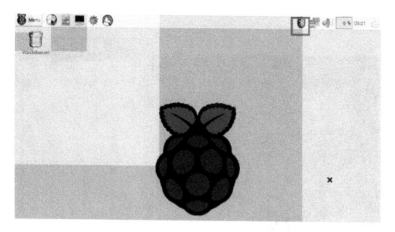

Circuit Diagram:

Circuit outline for this Raspberry Pi based Bluetooth Controlled Home Automation is extremely basic, we simply associated Relay Module's information signal Pin to PIN 40 (GPIO 21) of Raspberry Pi as well as other 2 Pin (Vcc as well as GND of transfer module) to Pin two as well as six of Raspberry Pi three. At that point we have associated an AC CFL bulb to the Relay as appeared in the circuit outline:

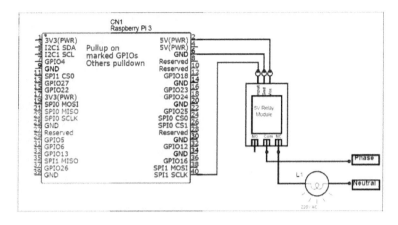

In the event that you are new to Relay and need to study Relay and its associations with AC machine, check this Article.

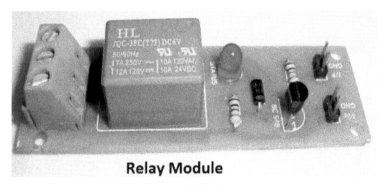

Relay Module

6v Relay Module

Controlling AC Appliance with Android App Blue-Term:

Presently in the wake of paring the Mobile Phone, we have to introduce an Android App for speaking with Raspberry Pi utilizing a Bluetooth Serial Adapter, so we can control the GPIO pins of Raspberry Pi. As told before RFCOMM/SPP convention copies sequential correspondence over Bluetooth, so we introduced here BlueTerm App which bolsters this convention.

Terminal emulator to connect to any serial
device with bluetooth serial adapter.

You can likewise utilize some other Bluetooth Terminal App which underpins correspondence by means of RFCOMM attachment.

Presently in the wake of downloading and introducing the BlueTerm App, run the beneath given Python Program from the terminal and interface the matched raspberrypi gadget from the BlueTerm App simultaneously.

After fruitful association you will see con-nected:raspberrypi at the upper right corner of the App as demonstrated as follows:

Presently you can simply enter '1' or '0' from the BlueTerm application to make the GPIO pin HIGH as well as LOW individually, which in turns triggers the Relay module associated with this pin, which further controls the AC bulb associated with Relay. Press 'q' to leave the program. You can utilize Google Voice Typing Keyboard to manage the GPIO utilizing your Voice.

So this is the means by which you can remotely control the AC Appliance utilizing an Android App over Bluetooth. Additionally check How to utilize Bluetooth with Arduino.

Programming Explanation:

Python Program for Managing Raspberry Pi GPIO with Android App is basic and plain as day. Just we have to adapt tad about the code identified with Bluetooth RFCOMM correspondence. First we have to import the Bluetooth attachment library which empowers us to control Bluetooth with Python language; we have introduced the library for the equivalent in the past segment.

```
import Bluetooth
```

The following is the code liable for Bluetooth correspondence:

```
server_socket=bluetooth.Bluetooth-
Socket( bluetooth.RFCOMM )

port = 1

server_socket.bind(("",port))

server_socket.listen(1)

client_socket,address = server_socket.accept()

print "Accepted connection from ",address

while 1:
```

```
data = client_socket.recv(1024)
```

Here we can comprehend them line by line:

server_socket=bluetooth.Bluetooth-Socket(bluetooth.RFCOMM): Creating attachment for Bluetooth RFCOMM correspondence.

server_socket.bind(("", port):- Server ties the content on have " to port.

server_socket.listen(1): Server tunes in to acknowledge each association in turn.

client_socket, address = server_socket.accept(): Server acknowledges customer's association ask for and dole out the macintosh address to the variable location, client_socket is the customer's attachment

information = client_socket.recv(1024): Receive information through the customer attachment client_socket and appoint it to the variable information. Greatest 1024 characters can be gotten at once.

At last after all the programming, close the customer and server association utilizing beneath code:

```
client_socket.close()

server_socket.close()
```

The various code is simple and clear as crystal. Check the full code underneath. Attempt to alter this task and you can utilize it to control numerous different things remotely, Robot vehicle through android telephone or can utilize your voice to control the lights.

Likewise check our numerous kinds of Home Automations Projects utilizing various advancements and Microcontrollers like:

- DTMF Based Home Automation

- GSM Based Home Automation utilizing Arduino

- PC Controlled Home Automation utilizing Arduino

- Bluetooth Controlled Home Automation utilizing 8051

- IR Remote Controlled Home Automation utilizing Arduino

- home computerization venture utilizing MATLAB and Arduino

- RF Remote Controlled LEDs Using Raspberry Pi

- Advanced mobile phone Controlled Home Automation utilizing Arduino

- Voice Controlled Home Automation utilizing ESP8266 as well as Android App

- RF based Home Appliances System without Microcontroller

Code

```
import bluetooth
import RPi.GPIO as GPIO    #calling for header file which helps in using GPIOs of PI
BULB=21


GPIO.setmode(GPIO.BCM)    #programming the GPIO by BCM pin numbers. (like PIN40 as GPIO21)
GPIO.setwarnings(False)
GPIO.setup(BULB,GPIO.OUT)    #initialize  GPIO21 (Relay connected at this pin) as an output Pin
GPIO.output(BULB,0)


server_socket=bluetooth.BluetoothSocket(bluetooth.RFCOMM)


port = 1
server_socket.bind(("",port))
server_socket.listen(1)
```

```
client_socket,address = server_socket.accept()
print "Accepted connection from ",address
while 1:


 data = client_socket.recv(1024)
 print "Received: %s" % data
 if (data == "0"):  #if '0' is sent from the Android App,
turn OFF the CFL bulb
 print ("AC light OFF")
 GPIO.output(BULB,0)
 if (data == "1"):  #if '1' is sent from the Android App,
turn OFF the CFL bulb
 print ("AC light ON")
 GPIO.output(BULB,1)
 if (data == "q"):
 print ("Quit")
 break


client_socket.close()
server_socket.close()
```

8. RASPBERRY PI MOTION SENSOR ALARM UTILIZING PIR SENSOR

Security frameworks assume a significant job in our everyday lives and there we can discover many sorts of security frameworks with various types of advancements and with various value go. Being an electronic eager you can make a basic security framework by spending scarcely any bucks and some extra time. Here in this article I am sharing a DIY manual for make a basic Raspberry pi and PIR sensor based movement finder caution which will turn on the bell when the PIR sensor recognizes any human development in the zone. We likewise secured a straightforward PIR sensor based movement identifier circuit in one of our past articles where we secured the working of PIR sensor in detail.

Components Required

- Raspberry Pi three (any model)

- Buzzer
- PIR Sensor
- Connecting wires
- Breadboard

Working of PIR sensor

Detached Infrared (PIR) sensor is called uninvolved on the grounds that it gets infrared, not transmits. Fundamentally it identifies any adjustment in heat, and at whatever point it recognizes any change, its yield PIN shifts out to be HIGH. They are likewise alluded as Pyroelectric or IR movement sensors.

Here we should take note of that each item discharges some measure of infrared when warmed. Human likewise produces infrared in view of body heat. PIR sensors can recognize limited quantity of variety in infrared. At whatever point an item goes through the sensor extend, it produces infrared due to the grinding among air and object, and get captured by PIR.

The principle part of PIR sensor is Pyroelectric sensor appeared in figure (rectangular precious stone behind the plastic top). Alongside this, BISS0001 ("Micro Power PIR Motion Detector IC"), a few resistors, capacitors and different parts used to fabricate PIR sensor. BISS0001 IC take the contribution from sensor and does handling to make the yield pin HIGH or LOW likewise.

Pyroelectric sensor partition in two parts, when there is no movement, the two parts stay in same state, implies the two detects a similar degree of infrared. When someone enters in first a large portion of, the infrared degree of one half gets more noteworthy than other, and this causes PIRs to respond and makes the yield pin high.

Pyroelectric sensor is secured by a plastic top, which has cluster of numerous Fresnel Lens inside. These focal points are bended in such a way thus, that sensor can cover a wide range.

Circuit Diagram for Raspberry Pi and PIR Sensor based Motion Detector

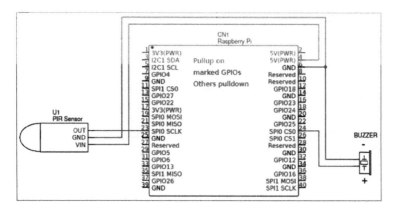

As appeared in the above schematic chart for Raspberry Pi and PIR sensor based movement indicator, the positive pin of PIR sensor is associated with the pin 4 (5v) and ground pin of PIR sensor is associated with Pin 6 (Ground) of Raspberry Pi (You can discover here the Pin Diagram of Raspberry Pi). The yield pin of PIR sensor is associated with the GPIO 23 of Raspberry pi which is utilized to offer contribution to Raspberry Pi. The GPIO pin 24 which is pronounced here for yield is associated with positive of bell, and ground of signal is associated with the ground (pin 6) of raspberry pi.

Python Code for Raspberry Pi:

The Python code for this raspberry pi and PIR sensor based movement finder is very basic and could be seen effectively with the code segment beneath. I proclaimed the GPIO pin 23 and 24 as info and yield pins.

```
while True:

  if GPIO.input(23): #If there is a movement, PIR
  sensor gives input to GPIO23

    GPIO.output(24, True) #Output given to Buzzer
    through GPIO24

    time.sleep(1) #Buzzer turns on for 1 second

    GPIO.output(24, False)
```

'Some time' circle is utilized as 'Genuine' so the substance inside the circle will consistently execute. in the event that GPIO.input(23): proclamation identifies if GPIO pin 23 is high, and if the equivalent is genuine it makes the yield PIN 24 high. The capacity time.sleep(secs) is utilized to stop the program in python for specific time where 'secs' is the time in short order. So here we used to delay it for 1 second. In the following line we made the yield on 24 as bogus so signal stops until the circle starts the following cycle, as While circle is set in every case valid with no precondition.
Code

```
#Raspberry Pi Motion Detector Code
import RPi.GPIO as GPIO
import time
GPIO.setmode(GPIO.BCM)
GPIO.setup(23, GPIO.IN)
GPIO.setup(24, GPIO.OUT)
while True:
 if GPIO.input(23): #If there is a movement, PIR sensor
gives input to GPIO 23
    GPIO.output(24, True) #Output given to Buzzer
through GPIO 24
   time.sleep(1) #Buzzer turns on for 1 second
   GPIO.output(24, False)
   time.sleep(5)
 time.sleep(0.1)
```

❖ ❖ ❖

9. DIY RASPBERRY PI TORRENTBOX: QUICKLY TURN YOUR RASPBERRY PI INTO AN ALWAYS ON TORRENTBOX

Raspberry Pi
Torrent Box

Downloading and seeding Torrents from the PC or some other committed server devours an extremely considerable measure of vitality, in the event that you are seeding it 24x7. Furthermore, it's likewise not defended to put the workstation on all the opportunity to simply download the Torrent. So here our Pocket measured PC comes into picture: Raspberry Pi. It is an ideal decision for Torrent box as it devours next to no measure of intensity and can be stayed on for long time. So you can have a modest Torrent Box running constantly in a unimportant running cost, downloading downpours for you. You can likewise run some different projects which require Raspberry Pi to be on for long time, similar to you can utilize it as Motion catch observation camera and can download the deluge simultaneously. So we should begin!

There are fundamentally two most prevalent answers for downloading Torrents in Linux System

(Raspberry Pi): Transmission and Deluge. Here in this Tutorial I am utilizing Transmission, as I thought that it was more straightforward, lighter and simpler than Deluge. Here is the little correlation:

Transmission versus Deluge:

As referenced before that Transmission is straightforward and light weight downpour customer in correlation with Deluge. Then again Deluge has more component yet minimal heavier, however you won't feel any additional heap on PC as PCs are a lot quicker today.

Transmission accompanies Web Interface out of the container, through which you can get to the deluges on the Desktop, just as on Smartphones utilizing the internet browser. Storm additionally has Web UI however you have to download and arrange it independently, Deluge likewise has a decent downpour customer for work areas yet it likewise should be downloaded independently on work area. Aside from that, Transmission can deal with Torrent magnet interfaces easily than Deluge.

My basic role is to simply download the Torrents without messing around the setup and I would prefer not to introduce another Torrent customer on my work area (as of now have uTorrent), so I have utilized Transmission. The two of them are great and have fundamental choices like Stop, Start, delay or erase and so on.

Converting Raspberry Pi into a TorrentBox in Few Minutes:

As a matter of first importance in the event that you are a tenderfoot with Raspberry Pi, at that point experience our past Tutorials on Installing the Raspbian OS in Raspberry Pi and Getting initiated with Raspberry Pi. Additionally check our everything other Raspberry Pi Projects here.

On the off chance that you have Raspberry Pi model underneath than variant 3, at that point you may require a Wi-Fi dongle to remotely interface the Raspberry Pi to switch or you can straightforwardly associate the Raspberry Pi to switch utilizing Ethernet link. Raspberry Pi 3 has Wi-Fi inbuilt in it. Here we have utilized Raspberry Pi two Model B with a Wi-Fi dongle. So ensure that Raspberry Pi is associated with the web, either utilizing LAN or Wi-Fi and afterward pursue underneath steps:

Stage 1: First run the beneath direction to refresh and update the Raspbian OS on Raspberry Pi:

```
sudo apt-get update

sudo apt-get upgrade
```

Stage 2: Now download and introduce the Transmission utilizing beneath direction:

```
sudo apt-get install transmission-daemon
```

Stage 3: Now all we have to do a few changes in the setup record of Transmission. First open the design document utilizing nano editorial manager:

```
sudo nano /etc/transmission-daemon/settings.json
```

What's more, include the LAN IPs in "rpc-whitelist" setting alternative and set the "rpc-whitelist-empowered" to 'genuine' like underneath. This is the IP which will be designated to our Raspberry Pi by our Router.

```
"rpc-whitelist": "127.0.0.1,192.168.*.*",

"rpc-whitelist-enabled": true,
```

```
GNU nano 2.2.6              File: /etc/transmission-daemon/settings.json

"queue-stalled-enabled": true,
"queue-stalled-minutes": 30,
"ratio-limit": 2,
"ratio-limit-enabled": false,
"rename-partial-files": true,
"rpc-authentication-required": true,
"rpc-bind-address": "0.0.0.0",
"rpc-enabled": true,
"rpc-password": "{17ec5c84c40cd7ea2342dfe66870f7de9c039620pFBzlOJM",
"rpc-port": 9091,
"rpc-url": "/transmission/",
"rpc-username": "transmission",
"rpc-whitelist": "127.0.0.1,192.168.*.*",
"rpc-whitelist-enabled": true,
"scrape-paused-torrents-enabled": true,
"script-torrent-done-enabled": false,
"script-torrent-done-filename": "",
```

You can likewise observe some different settings like "rpc-username" and "rpc-secret word", this will be required to login when we open the Web UI in internet browser. You can transform them as needs be; I left the username to default and changed the secret word. Secret word will consequently get encoded when the document is spared.

Stage 4: The area of downloaded documents are characterized in settings.json record as demonstrated as follows. Default area is/var/lib/transmission-daemon/downloads

sudo nano /etc/transmission-daemon/settings.json

```
  pi@raspberrypi: ~
GNU nano 2.2.6              File: /etc/transmission-daemon/settings.json

  "blocklist-enabled": false,
  "blocklist-url": "http://www.example.com/blocklist",
  "cache-size-mb": 4,
  "dht-enabled": true,
  "download-dir": "/var/lib/transmission-daemon/downloads",
  "download-limit": 100,
  "download-limit-enabled": ,
  "download-queue-enabled": true,
  "download-queue-size": 5,
  "encryption": 1,
  "idle-seeding-limit": 30,
  "idle-seeding-limit-enabled": false,
  "incomplete-dir": "/var/lib/transmission-daemon/Downloads",
  "incomplete-dir-enabled": true,
```

To stay away from any "Authorization denied mistake", we have to ensure that the proprietor of these registries must be a similar client who claims the Transmission Daemon. The client, who possesses the Transmission daemon, is "debian-transmission", so we are making it proprietor of Downloading catalogs alongside the registries which contains settings document:

```
sudo chown -R debian-transmission:debian-transmission /etc/transmission-daemon

sudo chown -R debian-transmission:debian-transmission /etc/init.d/transmission-daemon

sudo chown -R debian-transmission:debian-transmission /var/lib/transmission-daemon
```

Stage 5: Finally start the Transmission daemon and

reload the settings:

```
sudo service transmission-daemon start

sudo service transmission-daemon reload
```

Stage 6: Now you are good to go to download your Torrent records on Raspberry Pi. Simply open the internet browser and enter the IP of you Raspberry Pi with the port 9091 like http://192.168.1.100:9091. You will be given Login popup where you have to type the equivalent username as well as secret phrase which we have set in Step 3. What's more, you have your Torrent UI before you like underneath:

```
http://IP_of_your_Raspberry_Pi:9091
```

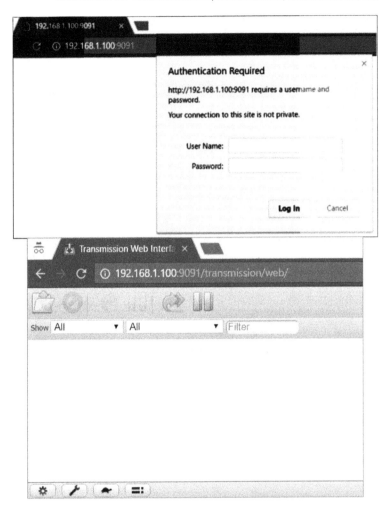

Presently Click on the Open deluge symbol in the upper left and transfer the downpour document or glue URL of magnet connect to begin the download. It's entirely basic as well as straight forward to utilize it, you will effortlessly get it.

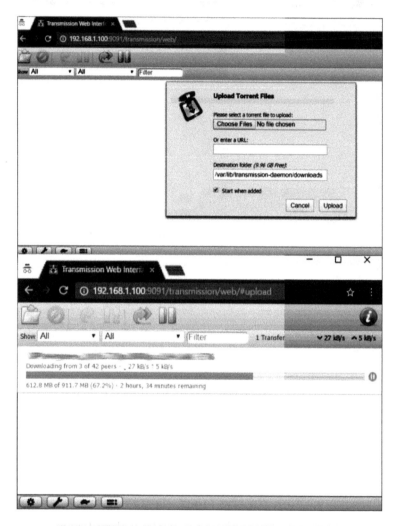

Transmission Web Interface on Computer

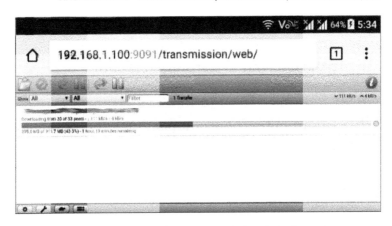

Transmission Web Interface on Android Mobile

This is same like some other BitTorrent customer and you can simply investigate the alternatives utilizing the interface. We can include, expel, plan the downpours and magnet joins works easily.

Stage 7: One last advance is to stack the Transmission settings on startup. In case Transmission, naturally, begins on boot and start downloading the lined downpours however the Web Interface doesn't begin consequently on startup until we fire "sudo administration transmission-daemon reload" order.

So to mechanize this thing, first make a document named "transmission-boot" inside/and so forth/ init.d

```
sudo nano /etc/init.d/transmission-boot
```

What's more, enter the accompanying content in that document:

```
#!/bin/sh

### BEGIN INIT INFO

# Provides: transmission-daemon-reload

# Required-Start: $all

# Required-Stop:

# Default-Start: 2 3 4 5

# Default-Stop: 0 1 6

# Short-Description: Reload the transmission-dae-
mon

# Description: Reload the transmission-daemon at
startup.

### END INIT INFO
```

```
sleep 20

service transmission-daemon reload
```

At last make the document executable and add it to rc.d by utilizing following directions:

```
sudo chmod +x /etc/init.d/transmission-boot

sudo update-rc.d /etc/init.d/transmission-boot de-
faults
```

Its everything done now, you can begin utilizing your Always-on Raspberry Pi Torrent downloading Machine.

Optional Settings:

Change Default Download Location:

In the event that you are not happy with default download area (/var/lib/transmission-daemon/ downloads) or you are utilizing some External Hard circle to spare the downloaded documents then you can change the download area utilizing settings.json record as appeared in Step 4 above. Yet, recollect that the proprietor of these catalogs must be a similar who claims the Transmission daemon to stay away from any Permission Denied Error, as clarified in Step 4.

Change Transmission Daemon client:

As we realize that the default client who claims the Transmission daemon is "debian-transmission". It is characterized in/and so on/init.d/transmission-daemon document as well as we can change the client from that point:

sudo nano /etc/init.d/transmission-daemon

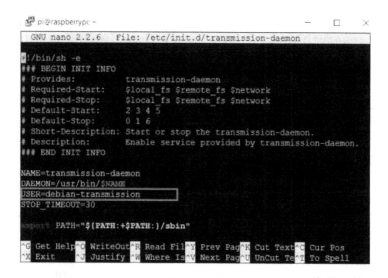

I left majority of the settings at defaults including this one as referenced before that I just need to download the documents and don't have a particular prerequisite. In any case, you can change this client to some other client like "pi" by altering the above record. Be that as it may, whoever the client is, we have to make this client, as proprietor of the indexes where the downloads will be spared and where the settings records are kept.

Likewise to change the client, we first need to stop the Transmission and afterward start it after the change by utilizing beneath directions:

```
sudo service transmission-daemon stop
```

```
sudo service transmission-daemon start
```

Set Download-Upload Speed:

There are numerous setup choices to control the Torrent like download and transfer Speed of deluge. We can restrict and set the download and transfer speed in the settings.json document like underneath. We can likewise change the paces structure the Web UI. The rates are appeared in KB/s:

```
sudo nano /etc/transmission-daemon/settings.json
```

```
pi@raspberrypi: ~
GNU nano 2.2.6      File: /etc/transmission-daemon/settings.json
    "script-torrent-done-enabled": false,
    "script-torrent-done-filename": "",
    "seed-queue-enabled": false,
    "seed-queue-size": 10,
    "speed-limit-down": 250,
    "speed-limit-down-enabled": false,
    "speed-limit-up": 100,
    "speed-limit-up-enabled": true,
    "start-added-torrents": true,
    "trash-original-torrent-files": false,
    "umask": 18,


^G Get Help      ^O WriteOut     ^R Read File    ^Y Prev
^X Exit          ^J Justify      ^W Where Is     ^V Next
```

Further investigate the settings record to transform it as indicated by your necessity. You can discover every one of the insights about the different choices and factors in this document here.

Unknown Torrenting:

At long last in case you require to conceal your downpour exercises from the ISP or some administration Agencies then there are different paid and free administrations to conceal you genuine IP address from others in the system. One route is to utilize some Proxy Torrent Service to conceal your IP as well as scramble the moving information like BTGuard, Torguard and so on. Also, other approach to utilize some VPN Service to course all you Torrent Traffic from the VPN, with the goal that nobody can see your genuine IP yet they will see the IP of VPN, as StrongVPN, Proxy.sh and so on. Thusly you can Anonymize Your BitTorrent Traffic totally.

So this is the manner by which you can change over your Raspberry Pi into low power Torrent Box. Check our other Interesting IoT extends here.

10. VOICE TYPING ON 16X2 LCD UTILIZING RASPBERRY PI AND ANDROID APP

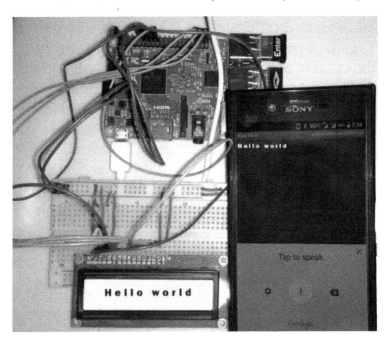

You should have acquainted with Voice composing, which is ordinarily utilized in Computers and mobiles telephone, where you can type any word by expressing it. Voice composing is valuable for crippled individual or for anyone who needs to type quick. We are actualizing the equivalent on 16x2 LCD Display, where the voice content will be shown on LCD. Here we have utilized 16x2 LCD, yet this arrangement can be introduced at numerous spots with a greater showcase to communicate any message, as at air terminals, shopping centers, workplaces and so on.

In this undertaking we will give the information voice utilizing Google Voice Keyboard through an

Android App (BlueTerm) and print the content on 16x2 LCD utilizing Raspberry Pi. Here we will type the content on 16x2 LCD utilizing remote Bluetooth Medium and will utilize USB Bluetooth dongle with Raspberry Pi. So fundamentally we need interface the 16x2 LCD with Raspberry Pi and arrangement the Bluetooth in Raspberry Pi to get the information sent by Mobile telephone. We as of now interfaced LCD with Raspberry Pi and composed an instructional exercise on Bluetooth with Raspberry Pi, you can check them.

Connecting 16x2 LCD with Raspberry Pi:

Before we continue with Bluetooth arrangement, first we will interface 16x2 LCD with Raspberry Pi. Here we have utilized an outer Adafruit Library for interfacing the 16x2 LCD with Raspberry Pi, utilizing which you don't have to compose numerous lines of code to drive the LCD and you can legitimately print on LCD by simply utilizing one line of code. Anyway this Library is made by Adafruit however it can utilized for any LCD module which has HD44780 controller. In case you need to associate the LCD without utilizing any outer library, at that point you can check our past instructional exercises to interface the LCD in 8-piece Mode and to interface the LCD in 4-piece mode.

To utilize the Adafruit Library, we first need to introduce it by utilizing underneath directions. First order will clone the CharLCD storehouse (by Adafruit) on your Raspberry Pi, second order will take you within that installed registry lastly we have to execute setup.py content, displayed inside the Adafruit_Python-_CharLCD catalog, to introduce the library.

```
git     clone     https://github.com/adafruit/Ada-
fruit_Python_CharLCD.git

cd ./Adafruit_Python_CharLCD

sudo python setup.py install
```

Presently the library for 16x2 LCD has been introduced and you can utilize its capacities by simply bringing in this library in your python program utilizing the underneath line:

```
import Adafruit_CharLCD as LCD
```

There are some model contents inside the 'models' envelope which is available in the library organizer (Adafruit_Python_CharLCD). You can check the arrangement by running char_lcd.py model content. Yet, before that, you have to associate the LCD pins with the Raspberry Pi as given underneath in the circuit chart in next segment.

You can likewise associate LCD with some other GPIO pins of Raspberry Pi, all you have to make reference to the right interfacing pins in your python program like beneath. Become familiar with Raspberry Pi GPIO Pins here.

```
# Raspberry Pi pin setup

lcd_rs = 18

lcd_en = 23

lcd_d4 = 24

lcd_d5 = 16

lcd_d6 = 20

lcd_d7 = 21

lcd_backlight = 2
```

Presently you can straightforwardly utilize the capacities gave by Adafruit Library to control the LCD. A portion of the capacities are given beneath; you can discover more in model content:

- lcd.message(message) = To print the content on LCD.

- lcd.clear() = To clear the LCD.

- lcd.set_cursor(col, push) = Move the cursor to any situation at segment and column.

- lcd.blink(True) = To squint the cursor (True or False)

- lcd.move_left() = To move the cursor to Left by one position.

- lcd.move_right() = To move the cursor to Right by one position.

Presently we will associate our Raspberry Pi with Android Smart telephone utilizing Bluetooth.

Installing Required Packages for Bluetooth Communication:

Here we are utilizing Raspberry 2 Pi Model B which don't have inbuilt Bluetooth, so we are utilizing a basic USB Bluetooth dongle for setting up Bluetooth correspondence in Raspberry Pi. You ought to have a Raspbian Jessie introduced memory card prepared with Raspberry Pi. Check this article to introduce the Raspbian OS and beginning with Raspberry Pi. So now we first need to refresh the Raspbian utilizing beneath directions:

```
sudo apt-get update

sudo apt-get upgrade
```

At that point we have to introduce not many Bluetooth related bundles:

```
sudo apt-get install bluetooth blueman bluez
```

At that point reboot the Raspberry Pi:

```
sudo reboot
```

BlueZ is an open source undertaking and authority Linux Bluetooth convention stack. It underpins all the center Bluetooth conventions and now become piece of authentic Linux Kernel.

Blueman gives the Desktop interface to oversee and control the Bluetooth gadgets.

At last we need python Library for Bluetooth correspondence with the goal that we can send and get information through RFCOMM utilizing Python language:

```
sudo apt-get install python-bluetooth
```

Additionally introduce the GPIO bolster libraries for Raspberry Pi:

```
sudo apt-get install python-rpi.gpio
```

Presently we are finished with introducing required bundles for Bluetooth correspondence in Raspberry Pi.

Pairing Devices with Raspberry Pi over Bluetooth:

Matching Bluetooth Devices, similar to cell phone, with Raspberry Pi is simple. Here we have matched our Android Smart telephone with Raspberry Pi. We have recently introduced BlueZ in Pi, which gives an order line utility called "bluetoothctl" to deal with our Bluetooth gadgets. Be that as it may, before that, interface your USB Bluetooth dongle with Raspberry Pi and watch that whether it is distinguished or not, by utilizing underneath order:

```
lsusb
```

Presently open the bluetoothctl utility by underneath direction:

```
sudo bluetoothctl
```

You can check every one of the directions of bluetoothctl utility by composing 'help'. For the present we have to enter beneath directions in given request:

```
[bluetooth]# power on

[bluetooth]# agent on

[bluetooth]# discoverable on

[bluetooth]# pairable on

[bluetooth]# scan on
```

After the keep going order "examine on", you will see your Bluetooth gadget (Mobile telephone) in the rundown. Ensure that your versatile has Bluetooth turned on and obvious by close by gadgets. At that point duplicate the MAC address of you gadget and pair it by utilizing given direction:

pair <address of your phone>

At that point you will be provoked for Passcode or Pin in your Terminal comfort at that point type password there and press enter. At that point type the equivalent password in your cell phone when incited and you are presently effectively matched with Raspberry Pi. We have likewise clarified this entire procedure in our past instructional exercise on Controlling GPIO with Bluetooth.

Circuit Diagram:

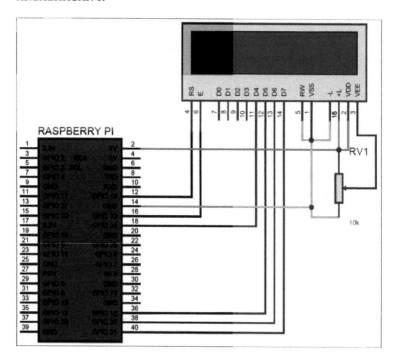

Voice Typing on LCD using Android App BlueTerm:

Presently in the wake of paring the Mobile Phone, we have to introduce an Android App for speaking with Raspberry Pi utilizing a Bluetooth Serial Adapter. RFCOMM/SPP convention imitates sequential corres-pondence over Bluetooth, so we introduced here BlueTerm App which underpins this convention.

BlueTerm
pymasde.es
3+

UNINSTALL   OPEN

100 THOUSAND   4.1   Communication   Similar
Downloads   1,255

Terminal emulator to connect to any serial
device with bluetooth serial adapter.

You can likewise utilize some other Bluetooth Terminal App which underpins correspondence by means of RFCOMM attachment.

Presently in the wake of downloading and introducing the BlueTerm App, run the beneath given Python Program from the terminal and interface the combined raspberrypi gadget from the BlueTerm App simultaneously. After fruitful association you will see connected:raspberrypi at the up right corner of the App as demonstrated as follows. Presently choose the Google Voice Typing Keyboard and start talking, it will be showed up the LCD.

Python Program for this task is given beneath and can be effectively comprehended. The principle run of the mill part is identified with Bluetooth Programming which we have clarified beforehand; check programming segment of this article.

We can additionally expand this undertaking by utilizing the Voice to control Raspberry GPIO sticks or can utilize greater LCD/TFT show for showing greater messages. Additionally check our past Raspberry Pi Projects.

Code

```
import bluetooth
import RPi.GPIO as GPIO    #calling for header file
which helps in using GPIOs of PI
import Adafruit_CharLCD as LCD
# Raspberry Pi pin setup
lcd_rs = 18
lcd_en = 23
lcd_d4 = 24
lcd_d5 = 16
lcd_d6 = 20
lcd_d7 = 21
lcd_backlight = 2
# Define LCD column and row size for 16x2 LCD.
lcd_columns = 16
lcd_rows = 2
lcd = LCD.Adafruit_CharLCD(lcd_rs, lcd_en, lcd_d4,
lcd_d5, lcd_d6, lcd_d7, lcd_columns, lcd_rows, lcd_
backlight)


server_socket=bluetooth.Bluetooth-
Socket( bluetooth.RFCOMM )


port = 1
server_socket.bind(("",port))
server_socket.listen(1)
```

```python
client_socket,address = server_socket.accept()
print "Accepted connection from ",address
while 1:


 data = client_socket.recv(1024)
 print "Received: %s" % data
 if(data != ""):
 lcd.clear()
 print (len(data))
 if(len(data) > 16): #breaking long strings into 2 parts
  i = len(data)-16
  a,b = data[:16], data[16:]  #first string will be of 16
char
 lcd.message(a)
 lcd.message('\n')
 lcd.message(b)
 print i
 print a
 print b
 else:
 lcd.message(data)


 if(data == "clear"):
 lcd.clear()


 if(data == "q"):
 print ("Quit")
```

```
    break

client_socket.close()
server_socket.close()
```

Thank You !!!